BENJAMINI. EAKINS. FILIUS. PINXIT.

AMERICAN ART IN THE MAKING

Preparatory Studies for Masterpieces of

American Painting, 1800-1900

David Sellin

Published for the Smithsonian Institution
Traveling Exhibition Service by the
Smithsonian Institution Press
Washington, D.C.
1976

Library of Congress Cataloging in Publication Data
Sellin, David.
American art in the making.
Catalog of an exhibition circulated by the Traveling
Exhibition Service, Smithsonian Institution.
Includes bibliographical references.
1. Artists' preparatory studies—United States—
Exhibitions. 2. Drawings, American—Exhibitions.
3. Painting, Modern—19th century—United States—His-
tory. I. Smithsonian Institution. Traveling Exhibition
Service. II. Title.
NC107.S44   759.13   75-45146

For sale by the Superintendent of Documents
United States Government Printing Office
Washington, D. C. 20402
Stock Number: 047-003-00037-7

SIP 6170

COVER: Marie Renard dancing el jaleo, by John Singer Sargent, ca. 1882 (cat. no. 60).
BACK COVER: Detail from *El Jaleo,* by John Singer Sargent, 1882 (fig. 97).
FRONTISPIECE: Detail from study for *The Artist and His Father Hunting
Reed-Birds,* by Thomas Eakins, ca. 1873 (cat. no. 47).
TITLE PAGE: Detail from *The Artist and His Father Hunting Reed-Birds,* by Thomas Eakins, 1874 (fig. 70).

Contents

Lenders

Albany Institute of History and Art, Albany, New York

The Art Institute of Chicago

Bowdoin College Museum of Art, Brunswick, Maine

Chapellier Galleries, New York City

Cooper-Hewitt Museum of Design, Smithsonian Institution, New York City

The Corcoran Gallery of Art, Washington, D.C.

Delaware Art Museum, Wilmington

Free Library of Philadelphia, Pennsylvania

Haverford College, Haverford, Pennsylvania

Historical Society of Pennsylvania, Philadelphia

International Business Machines Corporation Collection, New York City

Bernard and S. Dean Levy, Inc., New York City

Lyman Allyn Museum of Art, New London, Connecticut

The Metropolitan Museum of Art, New York City

Munson-Williams-Proctor Institute, Utica, New York

Museum of Fine Arts, Boston

The Museums at Stony Brook, Long Island, New York

Pennsylvania Academy of the Fine Arts, Philadelphia

Philadelphia Museum of Art, Pennsylvania

Smith College Museum of Art, Northampton, Massachusetts

Ira Spanierman, Inc., New York City

St. Louis Mercantile Library Association, Missouri

University of Kansas Museum of Art, Lawrence

Wesleyan University, Center for the Humanities, Middletown, Connecticut

Yale University Art Gallery, New Haven, Connecticut

Mr. William Morris Hunt II

Mr. and Mrs. Andrew S. Peters

Dr. and Mrs. David Sellin

Mr. Jackson Chase Storm

Artists in Exhibition

Edwin Austin Abbey (1852-1911)
Washington Allston (1779-1843)
Cecilia Beaux (1855-1942)
George Caleb Bingham (1811-1879)
William Merritt Chase (1849-1916)
Frederic E. Church (1826-1900)
James G. Clonney (1812-1867)
Thomas Cole (1801-1848)
Kenyon Cox (1856-1919)
Thomas Doughty (1793-1856)
Asher B. Durand (1796-1886)
Frank Duveneck (1848-1919)
Thomas Eakins (1844-1916)
Winslow Homer (1836-1910)
William Morris Hunt (1824-1879)
Eastman Johnson (1824-1906)
John La Farge (1835-1910)
Thomas Moran (1837-1926)
William Sidney Mount (1807-1868)
John Neagle (1796-1865)
Maurice B. Prendergast (1861-1923)
Theodore Robinson (1852-1896)
John Singer Sargent (1856-1925)
Christian Schussele (1826-1879)
Walter Shirlaw (1838-1909)
John Vanderlyn (1775-1852)
Elihu Vedder (1836-1923)
Benjamin West (1738-1820)
James A. McN. Whistler (1834-1903)

Acknowledgments

For nearly two years the Traveling Exhibition Service has worked to enrich its Bicentennial program with the development of exhibitions of American art. "American Art in the Making" is the most ambitious of these efforts. A loan show of significant drawings, watercolors, and oil sketches is increasingly difficult to organize, and requests for works of American art have been especially numerous during this period.

In view of these obstacles, we have been gratified by the generosity of museums, private collectors, and dealers in acceding to our requests. They have made it possible for us to assemble a group of works which fairly represent major currents and artists of the nineteenth century and which are happily varied in medium and theme. We have no illusions that the topic of preparatory studies has been exhaustively or definitively explored. We do believe that the works on exhibition make plain the wide range of approaches to the creation of works of art. They embody the freshness and vitality characteristic of the sketch, when the exhilaration felt by the artist in the contemplation of his subject is transmitted without concern for finish or completeness. Objects so instructive, and so handsome in themselves, cannot fail to stimulate the eye and mind of the beholder.—WILLIAM M. KLOSS, Exhibition Coordinator

Preface

"American Art in the Making" is a title that suits the double purpose of this exhibition: to present a general overview of the century that saw our art grow to full maturity and to offer some insight into the creative process through studies for particular works of special significance. This format also makes it possible to gather in compact form a galaxy of famous paintings, as represented by their preparatory studies, that would be impossible for any museum to obtain in the final state in this time of intense competition for American art. At the same time there is an immediacy, a direct experience with problems that engaged the artist, and a glimpse of how these changed during a single career or over generations. There are notable lacunae. Suitable studies by Mary Cassatt, for instance, were not available, and previous commitments or proscriptions against lending precluded gathering meaningful history paintings. Pure studio problems, like still life, also did not lend themselves to the sorts of studies produced for landscape or portraiture. Participating institutions might find in their own collections, or in those of benefactors, appropriate objects to augment the exhibition, and thereby eliminate some of these omissions.

Because of the sympathy and generosity of the lenders, public and private, this exhibition contains an extraordinary group of paintings and drawings. In the essay, I have attempted to put them into meaningful relationships within the context of American art. In the process of forming the exhibition I have had the encouragement and advice of many friends and associates, and to all of them, and to the lenders, I offer heartfelt thanks. —D.S.

Fig. 1. West: Composition study for *Telemachus and Calypso*, 1772. University of Kansas Museum of Art. [Catalog number 1]

Fig. 2. West: *Telemachus and Calypso*, ca. 1809. Corcoran Gallery of Art; gift of Bernice West Byers.

American Art in the Making:

Preparatory Studies for Masterpieces of

American Painting, 1800-1900

CLASSICAL BEGINNINGS

During the nineteenth century American painting grew to full maturity. By 1800 few mysteries remained in the art of constructing a picture in a traditional manner. Critical treatises, artist's compendiums and companions, practical guides to mechanical drawing, and artistic perspective were available to all, and engravings and illustrated books abounded, even if there was a paucity of original paintings of quality. By 1800 accomplished artists came to America, some to make a historical record of the new Republic or in the hope of receiving commissions for public monuments, some pressed by necessity to turn an aristocratic pastime into a means of livelihood, and others who saw a land of opportunity. At the same time the trickle of American artists who followed the lead of Benjamin West and went abroad to study became a steady flow.

Benjamin West departed these shores in 1760, never to return, but he always kept sight of his origins and of the needs of his fellow countrymen, who came in waves to his London studio for encouragement and instruction. After having imbibed neoclassic dogma at the very source in the Roman studio of Anton Raphael Mengs, and worshipped before the *Altar of Augustan Peace,* West went on to England and immediate acclaim. There he explored the concepts of Edmund Burke, and passed from the classical Stately Mode to the Terrible Sublime, the baroque diagonals, colors, and contrasts of Rubens. Finally, he synthesized these tendencies in a quieter classicism under the spell of the Elgin marbles from the Parthenon. Depending on when they came to him, his American students reflected each of these tendencies in turn. Matthew Pratt recorded the first of them in 1765 in his well-known painting *The American School* (Metropolitan Museum of Art, New York); the last survivors among his students, Samuel F. B. Morse and Thomas Sully, lived on until 1872. West's students founded our first art academies, recorded our history, became our first art historians, and some were among our best painters. Regardless of his declining reputation in England after 1800 and the disrepute into which his paintings had fallen in the United States by the end of the nineteenth century, West dominates art in the first four decades of the Republic founded in his native land. His influence was immense. Studies for four paintings by West, all in this country, are in this exhibition and trace his progress (figs. 1-7). The earliest, *Telemachus and Calypso* (fig. 1), is based on a well-known second-century relief of Perseus and Andromeda (Capitoline Museum, Rome), itself a neoclassic pastiche of an earlier era. West had anticipated the official style of France of the Republic and Empire, but *Death on a Pale Horse,* for which we have an early study (fig. 3), was done in pursuit of the Dread Manner. He sent a version of this painting to the Paris Salon of 1802, where it gained official sanction in spite of

towards the end of his life West was no longer a Roman but a Greek. The painting was in his studio when Washington Allston came to Europe for the second time, accompanied by young Samuel F. B. Morse, and Allston must have had it in mind when working out the first composition for his *Belshazzar's Feast* (fig. 8).

Allston and Morse attended séances held in London by the English artist John Martin, where electromagnetism was much in the air. Morse may have brought away some of his ideas for his telegraph; but Martin got an idea from Allston and asked if he would object to his doing a *Belshazzar's Feast* of his own. Martin's painting was exhibited soon afterward, with little critical acclaim but great profit to the artist from admissions. Allston never reconciled the frontality and isocephalism of the original scheme with new diagonal perspective schemes suggested by Gilbert Stuart, and the thing became an albatross, still unfinished at his death twenty-five years later.

John Vanderlyn was in the vanguard of an army of Americans indebted to France for their art training. He picked up the neoclassic baton dropped by West, and in Paris painted his *Ariadne* (fig. 10), which was well received at the Salon and caused a sensation in America when it became known that he employed live models. Our study (fig. 11) is a beautiful example of the practice of posing a model in a classic pose for later reduction to an ideal mold. The cast of the face and hang of the breast leave no doubt that the worst fears of the American public were founded on fact, if not cause for riot. In the final painting, Vanderlyn perfected the figure along academic lines dictated by ancient sculpture and Renaissance painting.

its heretical style. Actually, the composition is extremely controlled, and not that far from earlier works. Its play of lateral movement and pyramidal composition is well balanced, and it stands as a legitimate ancestor to Picasso's famous apocalyptic vision of Guernica. A preparatory study for West's *Burghers of Calais* (fig. 5) shows the same deft touch, and the spidery figure of a lunatic (fig. 6) was worked into a composition for *Christ Healing the Sick* (fig. 7), one of his best-known paintings in the United States. It had its own pavilion on the grounds of the Pennsylvania Hospital when not on tour, until retired to a corridor of the Hospital for the Insane. For the paying spectator there was a pamphlet explaining the artistic qualities of the characterizations, and the problems of color, distance, atmosphere, balance, and so forth. It pointed out that the isocephalism and friezelike effect came from contemplation of the Parthenon frieze, so

Fig. 3. West: Study, ca. 1787, for *Death on the Pale Horse.* Delaware Art Museum. [Catalog number 3]

Fig. 4. West: Early version, ca. 1787, for *Death on the Pale Horse.* Philadelphia Museum of Art.

Fig. 5. West: Composition study for *Queen Philippa Interceding for the Burghers of Calais,* the painting in the Detroit Institute of Arts. Delaware Art Museum. [Catalog number 2]

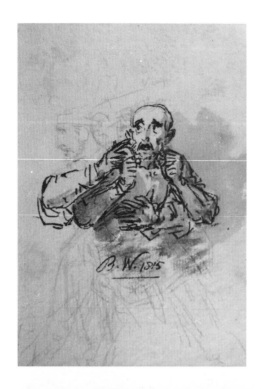

Fig. 6. West: Study of a lunatic, 1815, for *Christ Healing the Sick*. Delaware Art Museum. [Catalog number 4]

Fig. 7. West: *Christ Healing the Sick,* 1818. Pennsylvania Hospital; gift of the artist.

Fig. 8. Allston: Early composition, 1817, for *Belshazzar's Feast*. Museum of Fine Arts, Boston. [Catalog number 5]

Fig. 9. Mount: Composition study, 1828, for *Saul and the Witch of Endor*. The Museums at Stony Brook, Long Island. [Catalog number 6]

14

Fig. 10. Vanderlyn: *Ariadne Asleep on the Isle of Naxos,* 1812. Pennsylvania Academy of the Fine Arts.

Fig. 11. Vanderlyn: Life study in classic pose, ca. 1809, for *Ariadne.* International Business Machines Corporation Collection. [Catalog number 7]

Fig. 12. Neagle: Preliminary composition study, 1826, for *Pat Lyon at His Forge.* Pennsylvania Academy of the Fine Arts. [Catalog number 8]

Fig. 13. Neagle: Composition study, 1826-27, for *Pat Lyon at His Forge.* Historical Society of Pennsylvania. [Catalog number 9]

Fig. 14. Schussele: Portrait from life of Samuel F. B. Morse, ca. 1862; study for *Men of Progress: American Inventors*. Museum of History and Technology, Smithsonian Institution. [Catalog number 10]

Fig. 15. Schussele: *Men of Progress: American Inventors*, 1862. National Portrait Gallery, Smithsonian Institution.

THE AMERICAN LANDSCAPE

Artists who went abroad to study returned with the indelible stamp of their masters, but for those who chose to stay at home, success was in their own backyard. There had been a constant clamor from the beginning of the Republic for a distinctive national style. Audubon came from France equipped with the same academic preparations as Vanderlyn, but discarded neoclassic conventions to record American birds and mammals in an unorthodox manner that earned him international recognition and admiration. Catlin evolved his own practical manner to record the life and look of American Indians, and his results excited such erudite critics as Baudelaire. Edward Hicks was at least as good, in the same vein, as the Douanier Rousseau. But these are isolated phenomena.

The untamed Eden of the American wilderness, however, had a universal appeal. As early as 1744 an Annapolis physician, Alexander Hamilton, sailed below the crags and storm-blasted trees of the Hudson, and wrote in his diaries of the romantic and awesome experience. The Frenchman Chateaubriand lingered lovingly over long twilight vistas in the wild. But it is the hymns sung by the poet William Cullen Bryant to the American landscape that directly anticipated and inspired the brand of nature worship found in the first cohesive school of American landscape painters—the artists of the Hudson River school. Actually, they belong to a long tradition, which appropriately goes back to the Dutch painters of the seventeenth century, but their subjects are indigenous, detailed with loving respect. Of this group there is a very impressive representation in our show (cat. nos. 11-24).

Thomas Doughty is chronologically the first of these painters. "He was one of the earliest artists to make evident the charm of what is called the 'silvery tone', and to reproduce with genuine grace and emphasis autumnal effects," according to Tuckerman in his *Book of the Artists*.[1] His topographical paintings and studies made along the Schuylkill, Hudson, and Potomac rivers have an unaffected honesty that transcends his technical limitations (fig. 16). Like so many of our foremost painters in

the nineteenth century, Thomas Cole was an engraver by trade. Before trudging from Ohio to Philadelphia he had studied an English manual of painting, but it was the sight of Doughty's paintings in the Pennsylvania Academy that introduced him to the possibilities in landscape.

"Cole and Durand may properly be termed the fathers of American landscape," Robert Weir wrote in 1876. "They first effectually inspired the artistic mind with sympathies whose influence is still felt."[2] He called attention to the poetic sentiment in the one, and the sensitivity and refinement in the other. Cole studied individual aspects of nature with pen and pencil—trees, rocks, a vista—and assembled them in the studio in conventional compositions based on Dutch and English examples (figs. 17, 18).

Durand was more accomplished technically, without peer in America as an engraver. He had a complete grasp of classical, historical, genre, and portrait painting, and owned Vanderlyn's *Ariadne* (fig. 10), which he copied in oil, reducing it to its basic tones in order to make an engraving of it. So before joining Cole in the celebration of nature in its wild beauty, Durand was fully conversant with the traditions of the past, and was a competent figure painter, which Cole never was.

Cole's *Voyage of Life* was the best-known narrative series that he did, and in engravings, marble-dust copies, embroideries, and other media, it graced Victorian parlors. The same John Martin who gained from Allston's *Belshazzar* paid back his debt. Cole had always borrowed heavily from Martin's illustrations for Milton and the Bible, and continued to do so in *The Voyage of Life*. Cole's original concept is shown in the first oil studies, and makes an interesting contrast with the final paintings. The originals are naively direct and appealing in their interpretation, although some are followed rather closely in the final works.

In *Childhood* the river of life flows from a dark and mysterious source bearing the infant and his guardian angel into a light and verdant paradise, reversing an *Expulsion from Eden* (Museum of Fine Art, Boston) that Cole once copied from John Mar-

tin. *Youth,* as captain of his destiny, leaves his angel behind in quest of his dreams, only to find in *Manhood* that events beyond his control sweep him perilously along to *Old Age,* where the angel, who has never been far removed, rejoins him to introduce him to his maker.

In the fresh and unstereotyped original studies (figs. 19, 20, 22, 25), the dream of *Youth* seems as attainable as a visit to Brighton; the young sailor hoists his sale as a motherly angel waves him *bon voyage.* The angel in the final version casually casts *Youth* adrift with tiller but no sail, while he gazes eagerly towards a mirage as inaccessible as Xanadu (fig. 21). A boatman braves a storm-tossed sea in the first study of *Manhood,* an anxious angel watching from a headland, but in a later study that was followed in the final version, a raging torrent sweeps a fearful passenger through a wild and craggy gorge (figs. 23, 24). Having flown along, aloof from the

maelstroms of *Manhood,* the angel is on hand in case our protagonist makes it to *Old Age* and the tranquil sea into which life flows (fig. 25). The narrative cycle is a Romantic concept from the start, but Cole made the first appealingly earthy studies into a popular melodramatic success.

Durand's well-known *Kindred Spirits* (New York

Fig. 16. Doughty: *Harper's Ferry from Below;* possibly a study for his *View on the Potomac near Harper's Ferry,* painted in 1827 for the steamboat *Albany,* and now unlocated. Corcoran Gallery of Art. [Catalog number 11]

Fig. 17. Cole: Study for *The Mountain Ford,* ca. 1836. Corcoran Gallery of Art. [Catalog number 12]

Fig. 18. Cole: *The Mountain Ford,* 1836. The Metropolitan Museum of Art; bequest of Maria DeWitt Jesup.

19

Fig. 19. Cole: Preliminary study for *The Voyage of Life: Childhood,* before 1839. Albany Institute of History and Art. [Catalog number 13]

Fig. 20. Cole: Preliminary study for *The Voyage of Life: Youth,* 1839. Albany Institute of History and Art. [Catalog number 13]

Fig. 21. Cole: *The Voyage of Life: Youth,* 1840. Munson-Williams-Proctor Institute.

Fig. 22. Cole: Preliminary study for *The Voyage of Life: Manhood,* 1839. Albany Institute of History and Art. [Catalog number 13]

Fig. 23. Cole: Composition study for *The Voyage of Life: Manhood,* ca. 1840. Smith College Museum of Art. [Catalog number 14]

Fig. 24. Cole: *The Voyage of Life: Manhood,* 1840. Munson-Williams-Proctor Institute.

Fig. 25. Cole: Preliminary study for *The Voyage of Life: Old Age,* 1839. Albany Institute of History and Art. [Catalog number 13]

Public Library) depicts Cole and William Cullen Bryant in the midst of an unspoiled sylvan vale. His *Thanatopsis* (figs. 26, 27) pays homage to that poet with an ideal landscape based on his famous ode to nature. While Cole made graphic studies and added color, Durand was known for his unconventional and truthful record. In 1877 a critic wrote:

Mr. Durand treats a landscape . . . with such an honest pleasure in the harmony and beauty of forms and colors, with so much quickness of mind, so much catholicity of taste, that one is charmed by his recitals. If his landscapes do more than justice to the green color, it is only because he sees more in these colors than most artists see.[3]

Frederic Church carried lessons learned with Cole in his Catskill paradise into lesser-known reaches of the continent, and earned international fame for American landscapists. He accompanied Cole on sketching tours, working directly in oil like Durand, and mastered Cole's style (figs. 28-30). He

developed a fine color sense based on direct observation from nature. In a period hungering after picturesque voyages, Church then followed in the footsteps of Alexander von Humboldt, and gave the public a cosmic vision of erupting volcanoes and Andean peaks in works that were as convincing as the stereopticon views he used as aids, but with a

---

Fig. 26. Durand: *Thanatopsis*, 1850. The Metropolitan Museum of Art; gift of J. Pierpont Morgan.

Fig. 27. Durand: Study for *Thanatopsis*, ca. 1850. Delaware Art Museum. [Catalog number 15]

Fig. 28. Church: *The Ox-Bow*, 1844-46, study after Thomas Cole. Mr. and Mrs. Andrew S. Peters. [Catalog number 16]

Fig. 29. Church: *Scene in the Catskills*, 1851. G. W. V. Smith Art Museum, Springfield, Massachusetts.

Fig. 30. Church: Study for *Scene in the Catskills*, 1850. Lyman Allyn Museum of Art. [Catalog number 17]

Fig. 31. Church: Study of Chimborazo above the clouds, 1853. Cooper-Hewitt Museum of Design, Smithsonian Institution. [Catalog number 18]

Fig. 32. Church: Study of atmospheric effects around Chimborazo, 1853. Cooper-Hewitt Museum of Design, Smithsonian Institution. [Catalog number 19]

Fig. 33. Church: *Chimborazo*, 1864. Frederick Osborn.

glorious color and fidelity not then available in panoramic photographs (figs. 31-36). Church was skilled at keeping his distances in place through atmospheric effects, and he excelled in giving his works "finish," that detail and polish that was so admired outside of Barbizon. To increase the illusion of actuality and infinite space, he exhibited his works under strong illumination, as seen from a dark observatory, framed with plants that served as living *repoussoirs*. Spectators were offered opera glasses or tubes in order to enjoy each passage from one trail or path to the next. In an age of spectacular landscapes, those of Church were sensational.

In several versions of the volcano *Cotopaxi,* the artist abandoned conventional spatial devices used in his earlier work and common in the works of Cole—the foreground tree and deep shadow that were used to establish planes of relief (fig. 36). From steaming tropics and spewing volcanoes, Church passed on to the most popular hydraulic spectacle in North America. Others before him, including John Vanderlyn and James Hamilton, had painted Niagara Falls, but none had captured like this the

majestic horizontal sweep, the passage of the surging torrent at the top, to its precipitous plunge (fig. 38). Church dispensed with conventional solutions altogether in the composition of *Niagara Falls,* perhaps finding them unnecessary considering the minute inspection of parts he expected. Studies under various lights and seasonal aspects were made in oil colors, and his observations of falls and spume (figure 37) are recorded with the same deft touch used in noting Cotopaxi's murky banner.

Fig. 34. Church: Study of Cotopaxi erupting, 1857. Cooper-Hewitt Museum of Design, Smithsonian Institution. [Catalog number 21]

Fig. 35. Church: Study of atmospheric effects around Cotopaxi, 1857. Cooper-Hewitt Museum of Design, Smithsonian Institution. [Catalog number 22]

Fig. 36. Church: *Cotopaxi,* ca. 1862. The Reading Museum and Art Gallery.

The beauty and excitement that Church found in the tropics and arctic were sought by other artists in the American Far West. One of these was Thomas Moran. His teacher, James Hamilton, had painted Niagara and the arctic icebergs and aurora borealis, and was an admirer of Turner. Travels by Moran to his native England reinforced Turner's influence, but it was the earlier works that he admired, those closest to Claude. "The public does not estimate the quality of his work by his best paintings," he said, "but by his latest and crazier ones, in which realism is entirely thrown overboard."[4] Moran was an eclectic painter, a collector of styles, and his works at the 1876 Centennial exhibition were regarded as alternate lunges at Turner and Calame, the Alpine painter. If the wilderness paintings of Sanford Gifford gave his namesake Gifford Pinchot the inspiration to create National Parks, the great expanses of canvas covered by Moran with the dramatic spectacle of the Grand Canyon gave Congress the vision to approve them. Color studies and notations made on the spot have the immediacy of those of Church, but Moran manipulated the final work a different way in his studio (figs. 39-43). He regarded "sentiment" as the most important gift that an artist could bring to nature, and said:

My general scope is not realistic; all my tendencies are toward idealization. . . . A place, as a place, has no value in itself for the artist only so far as it furnishes the material from which to construct a picture. Topography in art is valueless. The motive or incentive of my 'Grand Canyon of the Yellowstones' was the gorgeous display of color that impressed itself upon me. . . . I did not wish to realize the scene literally, but to preserve and convey its true impression.[5]

Moran went on to say that all of the forms introduced into the picture were visible from a given point, but the relationships were manipulated for pictorial effect. "For instance, the precipitous rocks on the right were really at my back when I stood at that point, yet . . . every member of the expedition with which I was connected declared, when he saw the painting, that he knew the exact spot which had been reproduced." As for France, Moran thought that it "scarcely rises to the dignity of landscape—a swamp and a tree constitute its sum total. It is more limited in range than the landscape-art of any other country."

The school of landscape that started in the Hudson River valley continued through the century. A. B. Durand lived until 1886, Church to 1900, and Moran to 1926.

At midcentury the principal goals for young American painters seeking instruction abroad were Paris and Barbizon in France, and Düsseldorf in Germany. William Morris Hunt started as a sculpture student in Düsseldorf before going to Paris to be one of the earliest of the Americans to study in the atelier of the powerful teacher Thomas Couture, and then he went on to the rustic village of Barbizon and its most famous resident, the painter Millet. For years Hunt was the most influential force among Boston painters and collectors. Because Hunt is represented in this exhibition with a late work, he will be seen in another context (figs. 114, 115).

Elihu Vedder painted side by side with Hunt in France in 1867 and tried his hand at a few Barbizon subjects, just to show his friend he could handle the style, and then he departed for Italy, where he spent most of the rest of his life. His manner at that time differed notably from both the Hudson River and the Barbizon painters. By then all landscapists took their colors and painted the subject on the spot, collecting sketches for paintings to be finished in the studio. Some of Vedder's have a range of color sensitivity that he deliberately toned down in the final works for the sake of unity. In his autobiographical *Digressions*, he recalled that he went to see the mountains of Gubbio but found that the worst plan for seeing a mountain was to be on it, but he made some unexpected discoveries:

Near this spot I found a beautiful subject. It was one of those little hermit-like hamlets left over from the Mid-

Fig. 37. Church: Study of Niagara Falls, 1856. Cooper-Hewitt Museum of Design, Smithsonian Institution. [Catalog number 23]

Fig. 38. Church: *Niagara Falls,* 1857. Corcoran Gallery of Art.

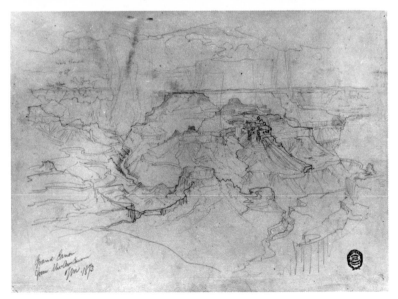

Fig. 39. Moran: Early version, 1872, of *Grand Canyon of the Yellowstone*. National Collection of Fine Arts, Smithsonian Institution; lent by the Department of the Interior.

Fig. 40. Moran: Sketch of the Grand Canyon with color notations, 1873. Cooper-Hewitt Museum of Design, Smithsonian Institution. [Catalog number 25]

Fig. 41. Moran: Sketch of the Grand Canyon from the Powell Plateau, 1873. Cooper-Hewitt Museum of Design, Smithsonian Institution. [Catalog number 26]

Fig. 42. Moran: *Mountain of the Holy Cross*, 1875. National Cowboy Hall of Fame, Oklahoma City.

Fig. 43. Moran: Sketch, with color notations, of the Mountain of the Holy Cross, 1874. Cooper-Hewitt Museum of Design, Smithsonian Institution. [Catalog number 27]

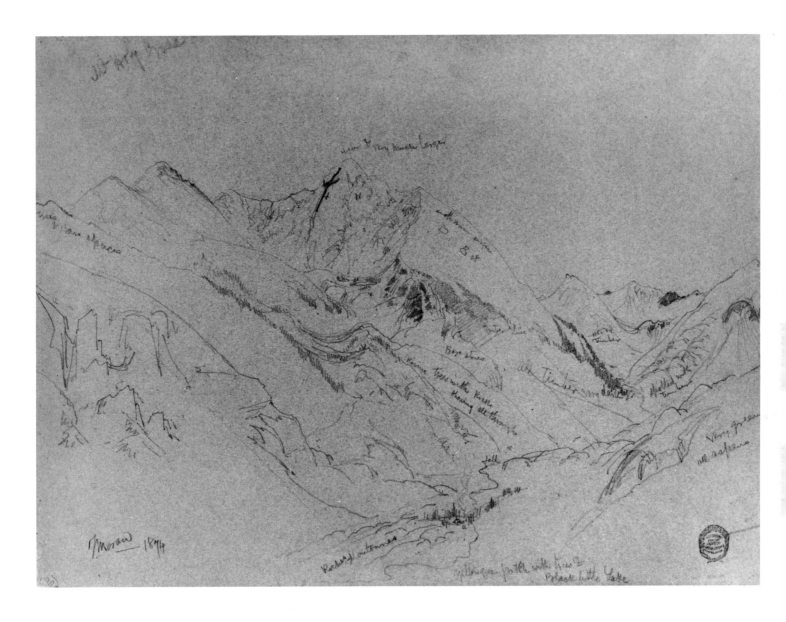

dle Ages; it had its strong tower, the houses themselves formed the walls, leaving in the center the usual piazza, and outside, the little church. All is up and down in that country, and so while crowning a hill it was far below us. It was evening; and so it was in a vast shadowed foreground, while the pale, barren mountains back of it had taken on a rosey glow. A slender thread of blue smoke rose from one of the houses—one evening meal at least was being prepared.[6]

By the World Forgot, he called it (fig. 44), and

later incorporated the study into paintings of the Umbrian landscape near Perugia. The simple planes of the shaved haystacks and stark walls, done in the fleeting moments allowed by the passing light, have the simple geometry of the views of Gardanne by Cézanne, who was just then beginning to come to grips with painterly problems. Vedder eventually took a different direction, however, and did not follow the course suggested by this work.

Fig. 44. Vedder: *By the World Forgot,* or Le Casaccie, 1867; study in Umbria later incorporated in *Near Perugia,* 1870 (private collection). Smith College Museum of Art. [Catalog number 28]

GENRE PAINTING

The academy and the studio of Emanuel Leutze beckoned from Düsseldorf to any young American inclined to study in Germany at midcentury. The Düsseldorf Gallery in New York was devoted to the promotion of that school of artists, and Leutze was well known in Philadelphia and New York before he went to Düsseldorf to work on his *George Washing Crossing the Delaware*. Some of the best American landscape painters to evolve outside the Hudson River school trained in Düsseldorf—Albert Bierstadt and Worthington Whittredge, for instance—but the training there is most closely associated with the painting of history and genre.

A position analogous to that held in landscape by Cole and Durand was held by William Sidney Mount and George Caleb Bingham in American genre painting—the depiction of scenes from everyday life. Each developed his style at home and found his subject matter in his own environment, even if Mount's early efforts were out of West and Allston (fig. 9). He soon turned to the familiar Long Island scenes (figs. 47-50). Bingham discovered his bent, as had Cole, on a visit to the Pennsylvania Academy, where he saw the genre paintings of the Swiss-American artist Krimmel, whose animated views of election day and Fourth of July celebrations struck a responsive chord. Back in Missouri, Bingham created some of his most thoughtfully constructed paintings on the same subjects. Mount and Bingham both depicted physical and racial types with understanding, and without condescension. Anecdote seldom took precedence over pictorial achievement, as it sometimes did in the works of contemporaries (figs. 45, 46), although the narrative element is an integral part of their work.

Mount conceived his compositions as a unity, and worked his details into them, constructing his space on a simple one point perspective (figs. 47-50). Bingham seems to have worked the other way around, with well-developed individual figure studies that he incorporated in complex compositions for which no overall projects survive. Like Mount, he favored a classic frontality, but was disposed towards pyramidal compositions (figs. 51-59). Bingham finally did get to Düsseldorf, but by then his finest accomplishments were behind him.

Fig. 45. Clonney: Composition study for *Mexican News,* ca. 1847. Munson-Williams-Proctor Institute. [Catalog number 29]

Fig. 46. Clonney: *Mexican News,* 1847. Munson-Williams-Proctor Institute.

Fig. 47. Mount: Composition studies for *Dance of the Haymakers* and *Power of Music,* ca. 1845. The Museums at Stony Brook, Long Island. [Catalog number 30]

Fig. 48. Mount: Preliminary study of *Eel Spearing at Setauket,* ca. 1845. The Museums at Stony Brook, Long Island. [Catalog number 31]

Fig. 49. Mount: Composition studies for *Eel Spearing at Setauket,* ca. 1845. The Museums at Stony Brook, Long Island. [Catalog number 32]

Fig. 50. Mount: *Eel Spearing at Setauket,* 1845. New York State Historical Association, Cooperstown.

Fig. 51. Bingham: *Fur Traders Descending the Missouri,* or *French Trader and Half-breed Son,* 1845. The Metropolitan Museum of Art.

Fig. 52. Bingham: Study for the half-breed son, ca. 1845, for *Fur Traders Descending the Missouri.* St. Louis Mercantile Library Association. [Catalog number 34]

Fig. 53. Bingham: Study for the French trader, ca. 1845, for *Fur Traders Descending the Missouri.* St. Louis Mercantile Library Association. [Catalog number 33]

Mount and Bingham had painted major works by the time the young Eastman Johnson sailed for the German art center on the Rhine. Johnson had some experience with lithography and crayon portraits, and had a good sense for light and shade, but in the Düsseldorf Academy and the studio of Leutze he learned picture making. Then he went for an extended stay in Holland, where Rembrandt and Hals were always before him, a reproach to tight brushwork and slick surface. A stint in the studio of Couture in Paris after that gave him an additional mastery of the painterly surface, of drawing with the brush and modeling with broad planes of contrasting value. Following a trip west to paint Wisconsin Indians, Johnson settled in his native New England, and found his subjects there (figs. 60-64). Like Bingham, he excelled in the individual figure study. His compositional studies are complete little works in themselves, unafflicted with the common complaint of "finish" that froze so many of the completed pictures of the day, including a few of his own.

Winslow Homer learned the lithographer's trade in the same Boston shop as Johnson—again the discipline of the print is behind the painter's art. Homer and Johnson both followed the Civil War battlefields for subjects, but they were not battle painters in the European sense, but recorders of events—reporters. The requirements of the wood engravings, the medium in which his drawings were made public, made Homer aware of the same sort of broad handling of light and shade and edge that engaged other artists of the time in the Boston of William Morris Hunt, the champion of Couture and Millet.

Homer was homegrown, like Bingham and

Fig. 54. Bingham: Study of a reclining figure, ca. 1846; used in several versions of paintings of raftsmen on the Missouri. St. Louis Mercantile Library Association. [Catalog number 35]

Fig. 55. Bingham: Study of a fiddler, ca. 1846; used in several versions of paintings of raftsmen on the Missouri, including *The Jolly Flatboatmen*, 1846, and *Jolly Flatboatmen in Port*. St. Louis Mercantile Library Association. [Catalog number 36]

Fig. 56. Bingham: Study of a Revolutionary War veteran, ca. 1852; incorporated into *Country Election*. St. Louis Mercantile Library Association. [Catalog number 39]

Fig. 57. John Sartain: Engraving after Bingham's *Country Election*.

Fig. 58. Bingham: Study of a toper, ca. 1852; incorporated into *Country Election*. St. Louis Mercantile Library Association. [Catalog number 37]

Fig. 59. Bingham: Study of a drunken voter and friend, ca. 1852; incorporated into *Country Election*. St. Louis Mercantile Library Association. [Catalog number 38]

Fig. 60. Johnson: Studies of corn huskers, 1876. Free Library of Philadelphia. [Catalog number 40]

Fig. 61. Johnson: *Corn Husking,* 1876. The Art Institute of Chicago, Potter Palmer Collection. There is a close variant in the Metropolitan Museum of Art.

Fig. 62. Johnson: *Nantucket Interior,* 1876; sketch of seamen's home, used in *The Nantucket School of Philosophy.* Wesleyan University, Center for the Humanities. [Catalog number 41]

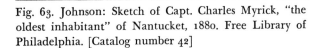

Fig. 63. Johnson: Sketch of Capt. Charles Myrick, "the oldest inhabitant" of Nantucket, 1880. Free Library of Philadelphia. [Catalog number 42]

Fig. 64. Johnson: *The Reprimand,* 1880; composition study or variant of a painting now unlocated. Bernard and S. Dean Levy, Inc. [Catalog number 43]

Fig. 65. Homer: Study of a lookout, ca. 1895. Cooper-Hewitt Museum of Design, Smithsonian Institution. [Catalog number 44]

Fig. 66. Homer: *The Lookout—All's Well,* 1895-96. Museum of Fine Arts, Boston.

Mount, but he had more opportunity in Boston to be familiar with French art, and a trip to France as a reporter for *Harper's* did little more than strengthen developed tendencies. His studies in this exhibition are all from a later time, when he turned from scenes of warfare and its peaceful aftermath on the farm, or of the schoolhouse or watering place, to the toils of the sea. These are not the gnarled characters so loved by Düsseldorf, the embers of retired sea captains of Eastman Johnson, but the robust types who harvested the sea in constant combat with the elements (figs. 65-68). A trip to the English coast, and residence at Prout's Neck, Maine, provided him with his themes. Frequently, his compositions are as unorthodox in relation to placement on the picture plane as anything done at the time in America (fig. 66):

A glimpse of the swaying upperdeck of a vessel; The sea, white in the starlight over the rail; and just under the ship's bell a lifted hand and rugged face—stern and weather-beaten like the brazen bell—with parted lips, shouting "All's well."

A crude and angular art, but classic in its dignity and strength. The figure, a little awkward perhaps, is a living, moving, breathing being, an expression of absolute reality.

The emotion which such a picture arouses is enough to make one abjure academic art forever.[7]

Homer was by no means aloof from outside influences, and the cut-off, up-front patterns of some Japanese print might have helped him in this composition, just as an Audubon print gave him the ducks in his well-known *Right and Left* (National Gallery, Washington). Even admirers among his critics thought that Homer stopped short of the mark when it came to "finish," and that he could have brought his work along a bit further. But one of his admirers was the greatest American academic painter of them all, Thomas Eakins.

Eakins's genre subjects are no less robust than Homer's, but his method was different. He left nothing to chance, but kept carefully hidden the strict discipline of his process in the finished works, so that sometimes they appear as casual as offhand sketches. Comparison of an early hunting picture, done shortly after he had completed his course of study at the École des Beaux-Arts in Paris, with similar motifs by Bingham and Mount is instructive (figs. 50, 51, 69). All three are beautifully resolved,

Fig. 67. Homer: Study, ca 1890; used in *The Signal of Distress,* in the collection of Cornelius Vanderbilt Whitney. Cooper-Hewitt Museum of Design, Smithsonian Institution. [Catalog number 45]

Fig. 68. Homer: Study of fishermen in oilskins, 1881; made in Tynmouth, England, and incorporated in *Fishermen Watching a Storm,* or *The Life Brigade,* in the collections of David Gray and Mrs. Philip Stockton, respectively. Cooper-Hewitt Museum of Design, Smithsonian Institution. [Catalog number 46]

Fig. 70. Eakins: *The Artist and His Father Hunting Reed-Birds,* 1874. Mr. and Mrs. Paul Mellon.

Fig. 69. Eakins: Study for *The Artist and His Father Hunting Reed-Birds,* 1873-74. Art Institute of Chicago. [Catalog number 47]

among the dry reeds of the wetlands near Philadelphia, early on an autumn morning.

Before touching the canvas, know what you are going to do, Eakins had been told by Gérôme, and the extent to which he planned his own work is staggering. The scene is charted in plan and elevation, with the exact placement of the pusher's feet noted on the deck of the punt. The exact length of the pole is measured, and the diminution of the grasses calculated by perspective protraction, as well as the position of the boat, for which the tilt caused by the pressure of propulsion has been allowed. The figures have been disposed within the perspective scheme according to the center line and vanishing point. Yet, with all this preparation, the artist keeps attention at the proper focal plane by eliminating detail in the distance that would not be visible to an observer focusing on the close object. This is academic painting at its best, for it satisfies all intellectual expectations, while retaining the freshness of an on-the-spot sketch of a sport popular among shooters and gourmets. Eakins reverses the usual process in that his greatest detail is frequently in studies, while finished works often have the effect of a spontaneous study.

He could do quick sketches, and usually did so to establish the main lines of his portraits and other compositions (fig. 74), but the studies of men and horses were based on exhaustive research in the studio and dissecting room. Just as his rivers are flat and ground planes solid, his figures can stand up. Billy Smith, the boxer, may not have a classic build, but his bones and muscles are all in the right place (fig. 73). It was Eakins who discovered—and explained in a scientific journal—the tendon in a horse's back leg that locked the leg in place for certain work. His cow pony won't pitch over headlong into the Badlands (fig. 75). Many of his oil sketches are squared for scaling and transfer to a larger composition, as here, a common practice throughout the nineteenth century, and a trick of the trade known to all the artists that we are discussing.

and it does not demean the two earlier men to point out the extraordinary command Eakins exercised over the tools of the trade in realizing an apparently simple picture. All three artists chose the most stable, frontal vantage point in recording their own familiar horizons, and each looked to the proper characterization of individual types in their natural habitat: a French trader and his half-breed son in a pirogue in the morning mists of the Missouri; a monumental black woman and her young charge spearing eel during a Long Island summer drought; an old writing master and his artist son hunting

Fig. 71. Eakins: Detail of figure 69.

Fig. 72. Eakins: Detail of figure 69.

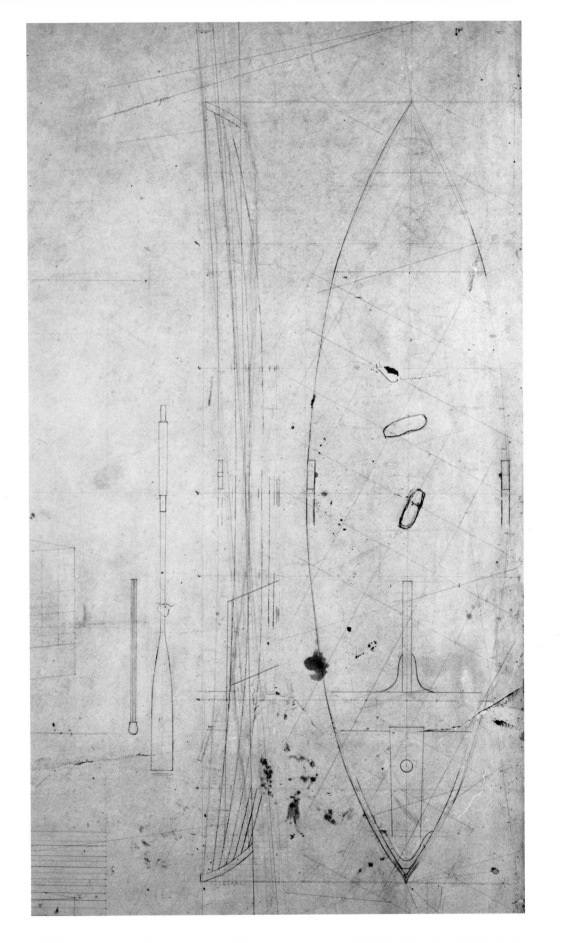

Fig. 73. Eakins: Sketch of Billy Smith, 1898, for *Between Rounds*. Philadelphia Museum of Art. [Catalog number 48]

Fig. 74. Eakins: Composition study for *Between Rounds*, 1898. Hirshhorn Museum, Smithsonian Institution.

Fig. 75. Eakins: Study of a cowboy and his horse in the Badlands, 1887. Philadelphia Museum of Art. [Catalog number 49]

1876 AND THE
NEW MOVEMENT

American art had entered a new era. It is always risky to single out one year as being critical in the development of a nation's art, but 1876 was a real turning point for the United States. In Philadelphia the Centennial Exposition brought together the greatest assemblage of our arts and industries ever seen, and these were proudly shown along with the products of other nations. Many of the paintings represented here by their studies were on view there in the United States galleries (figs. 33, 42, 57, 77, 84). Even at the time, it became evident to objective observers that a confrontation of generations was taking place, and that among the new men there was a clear division between two approaches to the canvas, originating in Munich and Paris.

The most conspicuous among the new artists trained at the École des Beaux-Arts were Philadelphians such as Thomas Eakins. The chief instructors at the Pennsylvania Academy after its revival in 1855 had been French—emigrés trained in the École des Beaux-Arts, like the professor of painting Christian Schussele (figs. 14, 15). His students were encouraged to go abroad to study, but not to Barbizon where Hunt's Boston followers gravitated. Instead, they went on to the rigorous grind of the Paris Beaux-Arts. There the program stressed complete command of perspective, tonal rendering with charcoal, knowledge of antique sculpture, and, above all, of human anatomy. Classical antiquity was no longer the envelope into which nature had to be stuffed, but was still a useful study aid. The aim was entirely focused on making the student the master of his tools, so that he might eventually be able to express what he might have in him. There were no geniuses.

In Munich the Bavarian Art Academy had flourished under Ludwigs I and II, and by 1870 had superseded Düsseldorf. Their programs were similar in that they were based on a course of studies with different masters, but there was an activity in Munich that was more congenial. Old tenets were being challenged in the aftermath of resounding military defeat—a trauma that Bavaria had in common with France. A group of young painters around Wilhelm Leibl accepted the realism of the older men, but identified more with Courbet, who had left a deep impression on a visit and languished now in exile in Switzerland. They also wanted greater freedom of expression than that allowed by the old history and genre techniques, and looked to the great paint manipulators of the past, Rembrandt and Hals, for inspiration.

Americans from the Midwest, with its heavy concentration of German immigrants, frequently had German instructors, and were inclined to go to Germany to further their training. A stream of very good ones ended up in Munich: Frank Duveneck, William Merritt Chase, and Walter Shirlaw, among others (figs. 76-85). Shirlaw followed the more conventional academic route, but Chase and Duveneck identified with the Leibl Kreis, and learned the techniques of modeling in planes of broadly applied strokes with a loaded brush on a tonal underpainting. Gone was the tight pencil drawing of the old days, and in its place a rough-hewn hatching or nervous freedom of line.

Painters of the seventeenth century were a source of continuous inspiration in the nineteenth. In 1800 Phidias and the giants of the Renaissance shared Olympus with the great Poussin, and Claude was synonymous with landscape; Washington ordered engravings after his work for Mount Vernon, and painters carried Claude Lorrain glasses—square mirrors, ground convex in black glass or polished stone to reduce a reflected view to its tonal values. Rubens and Van Dyck were a colonial inheritance from the English, and their Grand Manner conventions so conditioned official portraiture that even today we expect to see statesmen propped up by columns around which draperies billow before a distant view of whatever they preside over or hold dear. When he neglected to use the formula in painting a U.S. president, and showed Rutherford B. Hayes as an executive at work in his office,

Fig. 76. Chase: Study for *The Court Jester,* ca. 1875.   Jackson Chase Storm. [Catalog number 51]

Fig. 77. Chase: *The Court Jester: Keying Up,* 1875. Pennsylvania Academy of the Fine Arts; gift of Chapellier Galleries.

Fig. 78. Chase: Composition study with jester serenading a cockatoo, ca. 1875. Jackson Chase Storm. Catalog number 53]

Fig. 79. Duveneck: *Turkish Page,* 1876; painted with the props used by Chase in figure 78. Pennsylvania Academy of the Fine Arts.

Fig. 80. Duveneck: Study of water carriers in Venice, ca. 1884. Chapellier Galleries. [Catalog number 54]

Figure 81. Duveneck: *Water Carriers, Venice,* 1884. National Collection of Fine Arts, Smithsonian Institution.

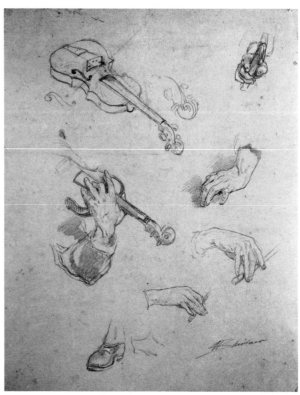

Fig. 82. Shirlaw: Study of a violinist for *Toning the Bell,* ca. 1874. Corcoran Gallery of Art. [Catalog number 55]

Fig. 83. Shirlaw: Studies for the violinist and bellmaker in *Toning the Bell,* ca. 1874. Cooper-Hewitt Museum of Design, Smithsonian Institution. [Catalog number 56]

Fig. 84. Shirlaw: *Toning the Bell,* 1874. Art Institute of Chicago, Friends of American Art.

Fig. 85. Shirlaw: Study for *Sheep Shearing,* ca. 1876. Cooper-Hewitt Museum of Design, Smithsonian Institution. [Catalog number 58]

Fig. 86. William M. Chase in his Tenth Street Studio. Museum of the City of New York. Courtesy Museum of the City of New York.

Fig. 87. John S. Sargent in his Paris studio, ca. 1884. Archives of American Art. Courtesy Archives of American Art.

Thomas Eakins found his commission discarded. Modified, the convention had been used by John Neagle even in a smithy, where he painted Pat Lyon at work before a distant view of the jail in which Lyon had languished as a suspected bank robber before vindicated (figs. 12, 13). The earlier study has the force of a Goya sketch, and it is interesting to see how the tools are then manipulated for compositional effect, leading the eye with punctuations until it became another conventional English portrait in the Grand Manner.

Although never forgotten, Rembrandt and Hals were being studied for newly discovered qualities of surface in Munich, and Vermeer was rediscovered in Paris after years of total obscurity. But it was Velasquez who suddenly came alive to painters seeking alternatives to the running battles between the Poussinists and Rubensists but unwilling to accept the rough-hewn realism of Courbet. Velasquez shone like a beacon from the Prado in Madrid, where most of his great works were kept, not the least of them that "theology of painting," *The Maids of Honor;* and his magnificent *Innocent X* was on public view in Rome. Whether in the stark realism of his early work, the optical truth of his spatial illusion, the masterful brushwork, or subtle control of surface pattern in the later paintings, there was something in Velasquez for every painter. Whistler found nothing incompatible in combining with Velasquez lessons learned from Courbet and Japanese prints in works such as the well-known *White Girl,* and these same influences are assimilated in his Carlyle portrait (figs. 90-94). Devotees of Franz Hals also admired Velasquez; William Merritt Chase copied the work of both men. A photograph of Chase in his New York Tenth Street studio shows him seated in his oriental corner perusing reproductions after the Spaniard (fig. 86), and he considered his major entry at the Centennial, *The Court Jester* (figs. 76, 77), to be in the manner of Velasquez. The walls of John Singer Sargent's Paris studio were hung with his own copies of both Velasquez and Hals, along with oriental prints, materials, and objects, while on display on an easel was his own synthesis of the three strains, the striking portrait of *Madam X* (fig. 87). Eakins knew the work of Rembrandt by heart, but the "big painting" of Velasquez provided the catalyst that freed him from the high finish of his master Gérôme and showed him the possibilities that he had known must exist in art but had never seen before going to Spain. Under the influence of Velasquez, he painted the great *Gross Clinic* for the Centennial. In the day of Art for Art, Velasquez was the artist's artist.

The National Academy of Design was founded in 1825 in protest against the moribund American Academy. Among its founders and officers were Samuel F. B. Morse and Asher B. Durand. Despite its name it was fundamentally a New York institution, although its annual exhibitions were widely supported by general submissions. Fifty years later the academicians found themselves being crowded off their own walls, and in 1877 enacted rules designed to guarantee their own preeminence in their exhibits. The young artists reacted by founding the Society of American Artists, with its own annual exhibition to be held at the same time as the academy's. The first one, in 1878, was a great success. The Beaux-Arts boys were well represented by Philadelphians, but Munich carried the day, as again the following year. The style had an immediate appeal because of surface brilliance and earthy subject matter, and was accepted by the public and younger artists alike. The Paris work was more demanding of the observer, but commanded the respect of artists. Critics were widely split, but never impassive. One thing that was universally recognized was the thorough professionalism and dedication of the participants.

What made the new influences permanent was the superior teaching ability of many of these painters, who arrived on the scene just as major new art schools were established. The Pennsylvania Academy was by no means a new institution, but the Centennial saw the completion of a brand new building, and with it a new program. Eakins aided the ailing Schussele as an instructor in the life classes and anatomy course, and even before taking charge as director in 1879 had made them more thorough than the ones in Paris on which they were modeled. In New York the Society of American Artists (S.A.A.) supported the new Art Students League, with Walter Shirlaw and William Merrit

Chase taking on teaching duties, so in New York the Munich approach was strong.

If there are regional tendencies discernible in American Art of the nineteenth century, I believe that they became pronounced about this time—at least for a while—in a Boston/Barbizon, Philadelphia/Beaux-Arts, Cincinnati/Munich/New York alignment. In any case, times had changed, and after 1876 there was as good instruction available here as in Europe, and the artists who went abroad to study did so out of choice rather than necessity. When they did, it was now almost universally to Paris.

English critics remarked on the lack of a salient American national characteristic in their reviews of the United States galleries at the Paris Exposition of 1878, the same year as the first S.A.A. exhibition in New York. While the French, German, and English exhibits were marked by some stamp of nationality, the United States collection was truly international, with each of the above styles well represented by painters as competent as their masters. This, perhaps, is the true nationality of American art.

The last quarter of the nineteenth century—the first of our second century as a nation—was rich in art. Abroad, our expatriates were in the mainstream of artistic currents. Whistler was an international character. Mary Cassatt was one of the impressionists, and Sargent exhibited with the Brussels XX. All of them submitted works to the first exhibition of the New Movement, along with Americans at home: Eakins, Sartain, St. Gaudens, Homer, Chase, Shirlaw, Duveneck, Ryder, and others. The tables were turned, and some of the old guard found their works rejected by the progressive Society of American Artists.

One issue burning bright in art circles just then involved the nature of light in relation to color. If blackness was an absence of light, did black have a place on the artist's palette? Was shadow an absence of color, or a color that reacted to the adjacent dominant brights? Goethe had long since explained the phenomenon of color in shadow, and the optics involved in what he termed "demanded" color, and what we call complementary color. Turner had understood and used his theories, but with Impres-

sionism it became dogma: black as a color had no place in the spectrum or on the artist's palette. Those dedicated to the tonal scale passionately defended black, and some who tried to adjust to the new notion were driven to distraction. Gérôme got so exercised that he would kick easels and generally knock things about the studio when it was mentioned, and his student Eakins thought that painting without black was like composing music with no base notes, pointing out to *his* students that the tones of paintings made out-of-doors had to be transposed, as in music, so that what was done there would look like outdoor light when seen indoors. Whistler's orchestrations were frequently based on black; he painted his mother as an *Arrangement In Grey and Black* and commenced a portrait of Carlyle as a second variation on the same theme, just two years before the first impressionist exhibition. Whistler had the reputation of having great facility, of being as quick and sure with the brush as an oriental calligrapher, a view that he fostered himself. But the effort put into his Carlyle (figs. 90-94) belies it. Carlyle was a neighbor, and Whistler put

the well-known face in its easiest cast. Likeness was no problem and plays the least important role in the composition, except as a "carnation" in an otherwise tonal painting. The writer sat willingly until he found that the coat was the main problem and, wearied by lengthy sittings, left it to be worn by a surrogate. The painting didn't suffer, and is more beautifully resolved than that of Whistler's mother, the coat and hat indeed being the principal dark pattern that plays the game of negative and positive shape, or field and ground, with the wall. The composition was first tentatively worked out in pencil (fig. 91), then in ink (fig. 92), and in oil (fig. 93); a croquis seems to be after the fact (fig. 94).

Fig. 88. Whistler: The Artist in His Studio, ca. 1867-68. Art Institute of Chicago.

Fig. 89. Whistler: Sketch in the studio, or *Composition II,* ca. 1865. Munson-Williams-Proctor Institute. [Catalog number 61]

Croquis du Portrait de Carlyle.

Fig. 90. Whistler: Portrait study of Thomas Carlyle, ca. 1872. Haverford College. [Catalog number 62]

Fig. 91. Whistler: Early composition study for *Arrangement in Grey and Black,* No. 2, ca. 1872. Freer Gallery, Smithsonian Institution.

Fig. 92. Whistler: Composition study for *Arrangement in Grey and Black,* No. 2, ca. 1872. Freer Gallery, Smithsonian Institution.

Fig. 93. Whistler: Composition study for *Arrangement in Grey and Black,* No. 2, 1872-73. Art Institute of Chicago.

Fig. 94. Whistler: Croquis sketch done after the *Arrangement in Grey and Black,* No. 2, ca. 1873. Fogg Museum, Harvard University.

Sargent shared a reputation for facility with Whistler, and he was as clever with the brush. His labors, at least in his early work, were as dogged as Whistler's in the effort to give the impression of effortlessness. His famous *Madame X* went through many permutations on paper before it ever got on canvas, and even then was a long haul—another great black painting. Sargent had studied in Paris with Bonnat, a great admirer of Ribera and the Spanish tenebrists, and with Duran, a champion of Velasquez and a convinced value painter, who urged his students to seek the demitint and work up and down the scale from there. In the bright sunshine of the Bay of Naples, or even in the pearly light of Brittany, Sargent had no difficulty finding blue shadows, and his watercolors are bathed in blue. But like Eakins he could not think of banishing black. Even when painting in Giverny along with his friend Monet, he asked for some black. When told by Monet that he had none, Sargent said he couldn't paint, and asked the Impressionist how *he* could do it.

Like Whistler, Sargent made one of his first important paintings from studies on a Brittany beach, when, during the summer of 1877, he painted at Cancale. Back in Paris, he worked up these studies into a major success for a young artist; his *Oyster Gatherers of Cancale* (fig. 95) was accepted in the Salon of 1878. All of the characteristics of the final painting are found in a smaller variant, the culmination of the compositional studies done in the studio (fig. 96). It retains the freshness of a sketch, but is darker in tone than the final painting, which is more given to blue in the dominant hue.

A trip to Spain in the following year resulted in a number of copies from Velasquez, on whom many of Sargent's important early works are based, and an introduction to Spanish dancing, in particular to the popular *el jaleo*. Sargent made sketches on the spot, and later in Paris he augmented these with studies of the dancer Marie Renard (figs. 97-102). Spanish guitarists and howling balladeers gradually took their places behind her in a stage space emphasized by footlights carved into the frame, and in 1882 *El Jaleo* (fig. 97) was a major Salon success.

Whistler and Sargent were international figures; Sargent the cosmopolitan sophisticate and Whistler the eccentric egoist. Whistler was the true expatri-

ate, but kept in close touch with American painters and patrons abroad, and of the two had the more profound influence. His contribution to American etching was profound. In Venice he came across the Munich crowd—Duveneck's boys. They were a congenial, young group, serious about their work and well grounded in the etching of Rembrandt, with whom not even Whistler could quarrel. Furthermore, they came out of a combination of realism in painting—including a respect for Courbet, with whom Whistler had painted in the early days—and Art for Art. This and their strong pencil work in sketching, when they pulled form out of the paper with blocky hatching, without teasing or rubbing of fussy outlines, made them compatible allies and willing students. In Italy Whistler borrowed their subjects, colors, and presses and enjoyed their camaraderie, while they drew from his store of experience and gloried in his eccentricities.

Thomas Eakins was deliberate and sure and was not noted for being quick. He could not paint a subject's clothing on a substitute sitter, and gave up more than one painting because of impatient sitters. Lucky was the subject who chose a sitting position, for those who stood faced an ordeal. Feeble old Walt Whitman had no choice, and sat for Eakins propped up by his window in Camden, New Jersey. A deft impression in oil caught all of the character of the sitter and the elements of the final composition (figs. 103, 104). The artist also made photographs of the poet to use as aids, showed him photos of Gérôme's work, and talked about art for art's sake while painting. Whitman was afraid he would look too glum, but came to see the portrait as a work of power and realism.

There were no copies of the old masters on the walls of the Chestnut Street studio. Eakins's "copies" were the casts he made of dissections and the photographs of his subjects. There was no place in the litter of armatures, clay barrels, sculpture stands,

Fig. 95. Sargent: *Oyster Gatherers of Cancale,* or *En Route Pour La Pêche,* 1878. Corcoran Gallery of Art.

Fig. 96. Sargent: *Oyster Gatherers of Cancale,* ca. 1878; final study for figure 95. Museum of Fine Arts, Boston. [Catalog number 59]

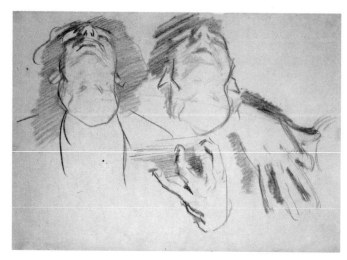

Fig. 97. Sargent: *El Jaleo*, 1882. Isabella Stewart Gardner Museum.

Fig. 98. Sargent: Composition sketch for *El Jaleo*. Fogg Art Museum, Harvard University; gift of Mrs. Francis Ormand.

Fig. 99. Sargent: Studies for *El Jaleo*. Isabella Stewart Gardner Museum.

Fig. 100. Sargent: Study for *El Jaleo*. Fogg Art Museum, Harvard University; bequest of Grenville L. Winthrop.

Fig. 101. Sargent: Study of Marie Renard dancing. Isabella Stewart Gardner Museum.

Fig. 102. Sargent: Marie Renard dancing el jaleo, ca. 1882. Metropolitan Museum of Art; gift of Mrs. Francis Ormond. [Catalog number 60]

Fig. 103. Eakins: Life study of Walt Whitman, 1887. Museum of Fine Arts, Boston. [Catalog number 50]

Fig. 104. Eakins: *Walt Whitman,* 1887. Pennsylvania Academy of the Fine Arts.

Fig. 105. Samuel Murray, Thomas Eakins, and William O'Donovan in Eakins's Chestnut Street studio, ca. 1890. Philadelphia Museum of Art. Courtesy Philadelphia Museum of Art.

Fig. 106. Beaux: Composition study for *Les Derniers Jours d'Enfance,* ca. 1883. Pennsylvania Academy of the Fine Arts. [Catalog number 63]

Fig. 107. Beaux: *Les Derniers Jours d'Enfance,* 1883-85. Mrs. Henry Saltonstall.

and easels for bric-a-brac or oriental corners. Walt Whitman and Winslow Homer would have been right at home there, and a photograph of Eakins with his friends Murray and O'Donovan (fig. 105) shows that, indeed, they were; Eakins's photographs of Whitman are pinned to the wall behind the bust of the poet by O'Donovan, whose portrait of Homer sits on the table, a prized possession of Eakins.

Cecilia Beaux, who had a studio next door, brings a number of these various threads together. Her first atelier experience was with the "Billy Girls," taught by William Sartain, Eakins's old school chum and fellow art student in Philadelphia, Paris, and Spain. Her Quaker family would not permit her to go to the academy life classes, but she gleaned what she could of Eakins's teaching from the "Boss's gang," as his students were called. Her first major composition (figs. 106, 107) was done shortly after the exhibition at the academy of *Arrangement in Grey and Black,* No. 1—Whistler's Mother. She wrote:

The picture I saw to do was a large picture, and I saw it complete in composition, the figures, lighting and accessories. I took an old piece of sketchingboard and did the composition small, but containing all the important masses, lines and color. The subject was to be my sister, seated, full length, with her firstborn in her lap. The picture was to be 'landscape' in form, and the figures were to be seen as if one stood over them.[8]

Never straying from the original conception, Beaux concentrated on posing the sitters in exactly the right position within an appropriate set. The focus was on the four hands in the center of the composition. Then she went to work. When an artist asked what she thought of when painting the child's legs, she responded, "Why, I thought about them." In the back of her mind, however, she never lost sight of Whistler's Mother in completing the painting. The end result is a pleasing blend of Whistler's surface pattern, directly out of his *Arrangement in Grey and Black,* and the solid modeling of Eakins.

The artist had never been abroad, but a friend took her painting to France and submitted it to the Salon of 1883, where it was accepted and well hung. When Cecilia Beaux finally got to France she enrolled in the Académie Julian for her first life study, and in 1888 summered in Brittany. At Concarneau

she tackled a major composition: two Breton girls on a beach, "the tones of *coiffe* and *col* mingling with the pale blue, rose, and celedon of the evening sky."[9] The painting is unlocated, but the final conception is in the studies (figs. 108, 109). The blacks and values of the early works have succumbed to the impressionist trend, which does nothing to diminish the strong modeling. In the nearby American art colony of Pont-Aven, Gauguin was painting these same Breton peasant types, still under the spell of Cézanne, but beginning to work out the symbolist-synthetist theories that would make the flat picture plane, outline, and local color areas his principal means of expression.

Another American art colony flourished in the Norman village of Giverny, whose most celebrated resident was Claude Monet. Sargent and Theodore Robinson, who had studied together at Duran's atelier, were there in 1887, along with Willard Metcalf, John Twachtman, and others. Painting with Monet, Sargent experimented with impressionist broken color and was inspired to emulate Monet by building a floating studio to paint on the water. On the Thames he later confronted Monet's subject matter, and wrote him of his "material difficulties of painting people in boats, on the water, between boats, etc."[10] Theodore Robinson worked on the same problems back in Giverny (figs. 110, 111). His results are interesting to compare with the solutions Bingham, Mount, and Eakins had brought to the same motif (figs. 50, 51, 69).

Photography had been used by artists for more than fifty years to capture likenesses and to reduce

Fig. 108. Beaux: Study with Breton Women and haystack, 1888. Pennsylvania Academy of the Fine Arts. [Catalog number 64]

Fig. 109. Beaux: Composition study for *Twilight Confidences,* 1888. Pennsylvania Academy of the Fine Arts. [Catalog number 66]

Fig. 110. Robinson: Photograph squared for transfer, ca. 1891. Ira Spanierman, Inc. [Catalog number 67]

Fig. 111. Robinson: Two in a Boat, 1891. The Phillips Collection.

Degas, Toulouse-Lautrec, and Bonnard, all of whom had drawn heavily from Japanese prints, Bonnard so much so that among the group called the Nabis, he was dubbed the "Nabi Japonnard." The new synthetist theories of Gauguin's Pont-Aven followers, and the work of the painters of the *Revue Blanche* and of the Nabis, were very much in the air. Content was stressed in varying degree, but all of these had in common an emphasis on the decorative aspects of line, shape, and color in relation to the flat surface of the picture plane.

Among Prendergast's first works after returning to Boston in 1895 were intimate glimpses of daily life in and around the city, of the sort that Bonnard had been doing in Paris, with no particular narrative content. Four of five variants on the theme of *The Breezy Common* were worked up in monotype from quick watercolor impressions made on the Boston Common (figs. 112-113). Painted on a hard surface in oil colors, the image is transferred to paper by pressure or rubbing while still wet. Thus the composition is reversed, and so is the usual additive process of painting in oils. Whites are achieved by letting the paper come through, that is, by wiping the plate with fingers or a clean brush, drawing with a stick in the paint, or by omission. With proper registration a number of plates can be used, but the usual procedure is simply to make the painting, print it, and reinforce with pencil. It has to be done fast, or the paint will dry. When handled well and skillfully, the monotype is a method that combines the luminosity of watercolor, the brushwork of oil, and the surface of a print. It offered the perfect means for Boston's own Nabi Japonnard to exploit the compositional problems of surface unity —field and ground, form and void. Overlap and diminution signal distance, but shapes stay at the

color to its values, as the Claude Lorrain glass had done earlier. Robinson chose a high vantage point and framed his subject in the viewfinder. Squaring the resulting print for transfer, he copied it faithfully but with the significant elimination of a boat. The zigzag pattern across the picture plane in the passage from one to another of the remaining boats emphasizes the flatness lent by the even texture and high vantage point. Manipulation of composition, hot shadows, and flat color areas are at variance with the tenets of Impressionism, but from here it is just a step to the early monotypes of Maurice Prendergast.

For four years, between 1891 and 1895, Prendergast studied at Colarossi's and the Académie Julian in Paris. He greatly admired the work of Whistler,

Fig. 112. Prendergast: Watercolor sketch made on Boston Common, ca. 1896-97. Museum of Fine Arts, Boston. [Catalog number 68a]

Fig. 113. Prendergast: *The Breezy Common*, ca. 1896-97. Dr. and Mrs. David Sellin. [Catalog number 68]

surface in *The Breezy Common,* unified by the mat, unvariegated green ground color, which is carried around the border. The printed word gives authority to the image and emphasizes the edge and flatness of the page. Whistler's butterfly seal has been brought along a little further, and cubists would soon take it from there, adding word association to their regular store of images.

Prendergast was by no means the only American exploring in this direction. By 1893 and the Columbian Exposition he had a lot of company. A great array of Japanese art was exhibited in Chicago, and original prints by Nabis, such as Vallotton, were published there; the *Yellow Book* and kindred publications were widely circulated, and the art of the poster was newly respectable. A slew of Americans were working on similar compositional principles in the early 1890s, the young John Sloan among them, but Prendergast was the master.

The public could hardly be expected to engage in such esoteric problems as those posed by Art for Art. But opposed to this trend towards individual pursuit of abstraction at the end of the century was an equally strong tendency towards a union of art and architecture—an American "renaissance" with a public conscience. In one sense the term renaissance is misapplied, since it was new to this part of the world.

ART FOR ARCHITECTURE

Our first public buildings in the new Republic suffered from misconceptions about classical polychromy, and what art was applied tended to be cut or cast in pristine white. Delays by Congress in commissioning paintings for the Capitol rotunda caused Samuel F. B. Morse to give up his profession, and soured the careers of Trumbull and Vanderlyn. By the time they got the job, their work was stilted and out of date. At the Philadelphia Centennial none of the buildings integrated mural paintings, although sculpture was conceived as part of the interior and exterior design of Memorial Hall, the art gallery that was planned as the permanent home of the new museum. Immediately thereafter, however, there came a change.

American architects, as well as painters, emerged from a thorough Paris Beaux-Arts training, completely familiar with the building styles of past great ages—ages that had integrated pictorial programs in glass, paint, and mosaic in their buildings. At the same time there was a growing conviction that the industrial era had plunged mankind into a slough of despond, and one of the means to elevate the human race was through art. Public buildings and places, as well as utilitarian household objects, should have decorative elegance and significance. On this premise art schools were founded in Philadelphia, Boston, Cincinnati, and elsewhere. The same industrial age had also created a new plutocracy eager to emulate the baronial splendor of their predecessors in their residences and "cottages." In this sense it was a renaissance, and Boston and Newport took the lead.

Among the pioneer mural painters were old hands like William Morris Hunt, John La Farge, John Singer Sargent, and Elihu Vedder, but new men like Kenyon Cox, Edwin Austin Abbey, and Abbott Thayer were soon among them. They would not have accomplished anything without the support of architects. In the forefront among these were Henry Hobson Richardson, Richard Morris Hunt (William's brother), and Charles F. McKim of the firm of McKim, Mead and White.

A place of honor in these endeavors belongs to William M. Hunt. In 1878 the Albany *Argus* reported Hunt's progress in the Assembly Chamber of the New York State Capitol, a new building by Eidlitz and Richardson:

Against the walls on the north and south sides of the chamber, some fifty or sixty feet above the floor . . . are the scaffolds upon which Mr. William M. Hunt, the celebrated Boston artist, stands to reach the large spaces (16′ x 45′ ea.) between the upper series of windows and the ceiling, which he is filling with two allegorical paintings. . . . The subjects adopted have been chosen with great care, having been sketched and done in colors, in various sizes, a score of times or more. They are appropriate in every respect, and will be finished in such a manner that New Yorkers may rest assured their ears will never burn at hearing such criticisms as are visited upon the decorations of the rotunda of the Capitol at Washington. . . . This work being all above the openings by which light enters the room, daylight does not serve for it; and Mr. Hunt and his assistants find the best time to draw their lines and spread their colors at night. . . . Then by the concentrated rays of the calcium light, the figures take form and life which soon shall delight the eye and promote the culture of every visitor to our magnificent Capitol.[11]

Hunt had studied sculpture in Düsseldorf before turning to the brush in the atelier of Couture. Among studies made for these murals are some very effective plastic representations of the horses that draw the moon chariot in his *Anahita,* or *The Flight of Night,* as well as pictorial compositions in oil and gouache (figs. 114, 115). For more than twenty years Hunt had been Boston's leading painter, and his brother the greatest of the Beaux-Arts architects. At last he had the chance to do big work, and he faced it with a sense of adventure, and with a pride at being among the craftsmen finishing the building. Alas, he had not prepared himself in the mural craft and painted his *Anahita* in oil directly on the sandstone, with the result that it became a ruin within ten years. He never did another, for the next year proved to be his last.

While Hunt was preparing his Albany compositions, his younger friend John La Farge undertook to decorate the entire interior of Richardson's Trin-

ity Church in Boston, recently awarded to him over Richard M. Hunt in competition. La Farge was an intellectual and an inquisitive person, a scholar and dilettante, before a brief stint with Couture turned him to the practice of art. He was well traveled among the churches and cathedrals of Europe, and was an admirer of French medieval glass. He read Chevreul on the subject of glass and color; copied paintings, particularly those of Rembrandt, in the museums; and was among the early admirers of Japanese prints. By the time that he tackled the Boston murals he was an accomplished easel painter, well known for suggestive form, subtle color, and a certain mystery akin to that of Vedder. His knowledge of architecture had been put to work by Richardson in the formative stages of the design of the Boston church, so when he was commissioned to decorate it he pitched right in, learned the methods and techniques of mural painting, and trained a crew of assistants; there were no Americans then skilled in the craft. Although his formal studio experience was sparse, La Farge had the broad understanding and fundamental knowledge of past styles of the most accomplished Beaux-Arts student, and he was quick to surmount practical problems. He launched the mural art in the United States. Nevertheless, it was in the art of stained glass that he made his most original contribution to painting and architecture, especially domestic architecture. Methods that he perfected led to a wave of similar productions by Tiffany, d'Ascenzo, and others at the end of the century. One of his most important commissions in this line was for the François I mansion of William H. Vanderbilt on Fifth Avenue, a large panel for a stair landing with the appropriate subject of *Commerce* (figs. 116, 117).

Fig. 114. Hunt: Study for *Anahita,* or *The Flight of Night,* ca. 1878. William Morris Hunt II. [Catalog number 69]

Fig. 115. Hunt: Study for *Anahita,* or *The Flight of Night,* ca. 1878. Pennsylvania Academy of the Fine Arts.

The study gives no hint of the color, but does record the composition, which leans on quattrocento models in style. Earl Shinn described it in about 1885 in a deluxe center-table edition commissioned by the owner of the house:

The stained glass windows, found on the first-story and second-story landings . . . are twelve feet in width. The artist is the well-known New York painter John La Farge, who of late years has almost abandoned easel-painting to give himself up to fascinating experiments in the manufacture and design of colored glass.

The subject of the first window completely occupies the space, with one harmonious, united composition. It is an allegory of "Commerce". We see the beneficent Power throned in the midst, with nymphs pouring treasure before her from cornucopias, or unfolding the masterpieces of the loom. At her feet is a river, the emblem of the carrying power of trade, with merry young Greek boatmen approaching in antique barges, hung with shields around the gunwales. The shields, the stuffs, the jewels and other treasures are so many pretexts for the employment of the most brilliant and original colors which glass can be made to yield. Jewels are represented by cut crystal, set in the leads, and shining with the full blaze of transmitted, instead of reflected light. Draperies and ornaments are made of sheets of unaltered glass, whose veining and variegation are done in the original manufacture: a mosaic of such fragments constitutes the picture, and by this means a burning glow and purity of color is reached, which painting on glass cannot possibly equal. It is really curious to see how the artist, in his truly inventive and thoughtful method, has avoided all of the pitfalls and inconsistencies of the European manufacture. Modern French stained glass is in stupefying contrast with modern French painting, being conventional, heavy, and covered with a pitiful mantle of poverty. Modern German glass attempts Rembrandt effects. . . . Modern English glass, obviously in a transitional state, does not sin by opacity, but sins often by the poverty of its tyrolike linear design, playing over thin, membranous-looking breadths of glass. The devices invented by Mr. La Farge have come to him after long study of those old cathedral "cartwheels" and "rosaces" to which time had given its magic of improvement. . . .

The balance of dark and light, as in all of Mr. La Farge's glass work, is kept half-way between realism and conventionalism: the windows are not too glaring, nor on the other hand are they darkened with paint like Munich windows, in the ridiculous effort to make a Caravaggio effect.[12]

If Boston's God required a Romanesque fortress, its intelligentsia sought a humanist monument. The Malatesta Library at Cesena was the earliest survivor of the great secular libraries of the early Renaissance, and by transference Alberti's great temple to the Malatesta in Rimini would serve nicely as a model for the new Public Library. Charles McKim did base his elevation on Alberti, so now mind and spirit face each other across Copley Square, appropriately housed. McKim designed the Walker Art Building at Bowdoin College about the same time. Taken all together these buildings contain a compendium of American mural painting of the nineteenth century which culminates in the Library of Congress. Both of the McKim buildings were well along and the murals underway by the time McKim, Meade and White formalized the American Renaissance in Chicago's Columbian Exposition, barely a century after Thomas Jefferson introduced neoclassic architecture to the new Republic and West discovered antique sculpture.

As a temple of the muses, the Walker Art Building took the form of Brunelleschi's Pazzi Chapel in Florence (fig. 118), and the subjects selected for the murals were Athens, Rome, Florence, and Venice. McKim had the advice of his friends Augustus St. Gaudens and Daniel Chester French in selecting artists, as he had in Boston. He also knew Vedder, who was the first to be commissioned. Of the Bowdoin murals, studies by Vedder and Kenyon Cox are represented in this exhibition (figs. 119-125). The subject Rome went to Vedder, the old friend of Hunt and La Farge. Allegory somehow made the nude respectable in an architectural context. The Pennsylvania Academy Life Class exhibition was shut down in the Education Building of the Co-lumbian Exposition, causing fury among Philadelphia painters—old students of Eakins. If nude pigs had been shown, Chicago would have rolled over in joy, they said, and pointed to the paradox of the nude allegory of Education that crowned the entrance to the very building in which nude studies could not be shown. Vedder's personifications at Bowdoin (figs. 119, 120) were done after studies from life but made over in his own ideal, just as Vanderlyn had idealized his *Ariadne* eighty years before, when Americans had been shocked to learn that women had posed naked. Now the nude was made the central motif in a conspicuous place in a gentleman's college. We had come a long way.

Both Kenyon Cox and Edwin Austin Abbey had been students of Christian Schussele before going to Europe for further study. Abbey went to England and fell under the spell of the Pre-Raphaelites; Cox followed the path Eakins had taken and went to the École des Beaux-Arts and the tutelage of Gérôme. Cox and the others who followed Vedder in commissions for the four Bowdoin lunettes had the composition fixed for them by his example: central figure, flanked symmetrically by various attributes. It is as formal and conventional as the old Grand Manner portrait, but somehow it works well in the architectural context. Cox did *Venice* (figs. 123-125). All of the lunettes were executed in the studio on canvas made to measure for the spot to which they would be applied, as they had been in Renaissance Venice. Hunt's tragedy would not be repeated. Cox made compositional studies in pencil and oil, and squared off individual details for enlargement and proper scale. For the personification of "Painting" he did a life study of a girl with a palette very lifelike, and then made her proper with drapery. Vedder blanketed his lifelike studies with the "Ideal."

The work by Abbey represented in this exhibit is not one of his Boston murals, but does convey his literary bent. His *Play Scene from "Hamlet"* is a very skillful work, and the studies are electric in their presentation (figs. 126, 127). The distraught Ophelia is studied individually, and the composition sketch shows the Danish prince reclined before the players, his head in her lap. The manipulation of the composition is as sophisticated and up-to-date as that of Prendergast, but there was some sacrifice to popular appeal in the final work, in which Abbey

Fig. 116. La Farge: Study for the Vanderbilt stained glass, *Commerce*, ca. 1885. Corcoran Gallery of Art. [Catalog number 70]

Fig. 117. La Farge, *Commerce* in situ, ca. 1885, from Edward Strahan, *Mr. Vanderbilt's House and Collection.*

SAPIENZA · PENSIERO · ANIMA · VITA · NATVRA · ARMONIA · AMORE · COLORE · FORMA

Fig. 118. The rotunda of Charles F. McKim's Walker Art Building, Bowdoin College. Lunettes, left to right, are Vedder's *Roma,* Cox's *Venice,* and La Farge's *Athens.*

Fig. 119. Vedder: *Roma,* 1894. Mural in the Walker Art Building, Bowdoin College.

Fig. 120. Vedder: Study for Anima, ca. 1893. Bowdoin College Museum of Art. [Catalog number 71]

changed to pink the white dress of Ophelia. The original conception would have shown her as though the *White Girl* of Whistler had sunk upon her wolf skins—a study in whites, played against the swath of red of the court figures behind.

Sargent's mural experience was limited to his student days in Paris, when he assisted Duran with a ceiling. Abbey had no experience, which he made up for by having a large London studio in which both he and Sargent could work on their Boston commissions. There, Sargent built elaborate armatures and stretchers to conform to the vaults and elevations. He worked out an iconographic scheme for the history of religion, and traveled to Spain, Cefalù, and Ravenna in search of ideas; he was already fully familiar with the great Renaissance cycles of Venice, Florence, and Rome. His lunette of *Hell* (fig. 128) recalls the mannerist work of Caracci or Giulio Romano, but for the *Frieze of the Prophets* his models seem more sculptural—a blend of the *Ara Pacis*, the Sluter *Well of Moses,* and Rodin's *Burghers of Calais* (fig. 129). The whole scheme was realized in the spirit of eclecticism that dominated the architecture of Copley Square at the end of the century. With these murals the century came full cycle.

Fig. 121. Cox: Life study for allegory of Painting, ca. 1893, squared for transfer. Bowdoin College Museum of Art. [Catalog number 72]

Fig. 122. Cox: Drapery study for Painting, squared for transfer, ca. 1893. Bowdoin College Museum of Art. [Catalog number 73]

Fig. 123. Cox: Preliminary study for *Venice,* ca. 1893. Bowdoin College Museum of Art. [Catalog number 74]

Fig. 124. Cox: Composition study for *Venice,* 1893. Bowdoin College Museum of Art. [Catalog number 75]

Fig. 125. Cox, *Venice,* 1894. Mural in the Walker Art Building, Bowdoin College.

Fig. 126. Abbey: Study for Ophelia in *The Play Scene from "Hamlet."* Yale University Art Gallery. [Catalog number 77]

Fig. 127. Abbey: Composition study for *The Play Scene from "Hamlet,"* ca. 1897. Yale University Art Gallery. [Catalog number 76]

Fig. 128. Sargent: Study of *Hell* for the Boston Public Library. Smith College Museum of Art. [Catalog number 78]

Fig. 129. Sargent: Study for the *Frieze of the Prophets* for the Boston Public Library, 1890-95. Museum of Fine Arts, Boston. [Catalog number 79]

THE END OF AN ERA

The sight of tycoons in silk hats emerging onto Fifth Avenue from Loire Valley chateaux sent progressive architects into fits of laughter—or ire. Beaux-Arts architecture was as much anathema to Louis Sullivan and Frank Lloyd Wright as Beaux-Arts painting was to John Marin, for instance. Still, the union of the arts that it engendered in the last decade of the nineteenth century was important beyond the limits of individual achievements. The same Chicago that saw the "Great White City" of the World's Columbian Exposition blossom and fade was rising out of its own ashes with a new architecture that would eventually destroy the magnificent mansions that lined New York's Fifth Avenue in the area of Frank Lloyd Wright's Guggenheim Museum. Wright was himself of the nineteenth century, and his Prairie House was a product of the Chicago exposition, where the Japanese pavilion transformed his approach to house architecture in a manner roughly analogous to the contemporary treatment of the picture plane by Prendergast.

The tendency among studio artists to explore abstraction to its outer limits led some turn-of-the-century critics to lament that there were no more thinking artists capable of finishing studies. About 1900 Sadakichi Hartmann wrote:

"If art continues in this weird fashion, it will soon be reduced to slips of differently colored paper, with a few disconnected, partly visible figures, sometimes only with certain parts of the body, like a knee or nose, appearing at the edge, or even merely with a few lines and dots and some crosshatching, that have some hidden symbolical meaning which one has to guess at from the shape and tone of the paper, the color and the suggestiveness of the drawing. Later on, as things develop, they may also perfume their paper, or exhibit strangely tinted paper with a childlike drawing consisting of two or three lines, or with nothing at all."[13]

The twentieth century was at hand.

NOTES

1. Henry T. Tuckerman, as quoted in Clara E. Clement and Laurence Hutton, *Artists of the Nineteenth Century* (Boston, 1879).

2. Robert F. Weir, *General Report of the Judges of Group XXVII: Plastic and Graphic Art. International Exhibition 1876* (Washington, D.C., 1880).

3. *New York Evening Post*, Nov. 9, 1887.

4. G. W. Sheldon, *American Painters*, 2d ed. (New York, 1880), p. 123.

5. Ibid.

6. Elihu Vedder, *The Digressions of V.* (Boston/New York, 1910), p. 426.

7. Sadakichi Hartmann, *A History of American Art*, vol. 1 (Boston, 1901), p. 194f.

8. Cecelia Beaux, *Background with Figures* (Boston/New York, 1930), pp. 90f.

9. Ibid., p. 148.

10. Richard Ormond, *Sargent* (New York/Evanston: Harper & Row, 1970), p. 42.

11. Quoted in Clement and Hutton.

12. Earl Shinn (pseud. Edward Strahan), *Mr. Vanderbilt's House and Collection*, vol. 2 (New York, ca. 1885), p. 99; photo 95: color plate.

13. Hartmann, vol. 2, p. 278.

Works on Exhibition

BENJAMIN WEST (1738-1820)

1. TELEMACHUS AND CALYPSO: Composition study, 1772
Pen and ink on paper, 12⅛ x 19⅜
University of Kansas Museum of Art, Lawrence; gift
of John Maxon in memory of John Wortham
[Figure 1]

2. QUEEN PHILIPPA INTERCEDING FOR THE BURGHERS OF
CALAIS: Composition study
Pencil on paper, 10¼ x 14¼ (sight)
Delaware Art Museum, Wilmington; Samuel and Mary
R. Bancroft Collection
[Figure 5]

3. DEATH ON THE PALE HORSE: Study for Death, ca. 1787
Pencil and wash on paper, 10 x 9 (sight)
Delaware Art Museum, Wilmington; Samuel and Mary
R. Bancroft Collection
[Figure 3]

4. CHRIST HEALING THE SICK: Study of a lunatic, with a man
in profile, 1815
Pencil, pen and ink, and wash on paper, 5½ x 3¾
Delaware Art Museum, Wilmington; Samuel and Mary
R. Bancroft Collection
[Figure 6]

WASHINGTON ALLSTON (1779-1843)

5. BELSHAZZAR'S FEAST: First full study, 1817
Oil on cardboard, 25½ x 34½
Museum of Fine Arts, Boston, Massachusetts; bequest
of Ruth Charlotte Dana, the artist's niece
[Figure 8]

WILLIAM SIDNEY MOUNT (1807-1868)

6. SAUL AND THE WITCH OF ENDOR: Annotated study, 1828
Pencil and ink on paper, 8 x 13
The Museums at Stoney Brook, Long Island, New York
[Figure 9]

JOHN VANDERLYN (1775-1852)

7. ARIADNE ASLEEP ON THE ISLAND OF NAXOS: Life study,
ca. 1809
Charcoal heightened with white on toned paper, 18½
x 23
International Business Machines Corporation Collection, New York City
[Figure 11]

JOHN NEAGLE (1796-1865)

8. PAT LYON AT HIS FORGE: Preliminary sketch, 1826
Oil on canvas, 9½ x 7¾
Pennsylvania Academy of the Fine Arts, Philadelphia;
gift of John Lambert, Jr.
[Figure 12]

9. PAT LYON AT HIS FORGE: Advanced composition study,
1826-1827
Oil on paper, 18½ x 13½
Historical Society of Pennsylvania, Philadelphia
[Figure 13]

CHRISTIAN SCHUSSELE (1826-1879)

10. MEN OF PROGRESS: AMERICAN INVENTORS: Portrait study
of Samuel F. B. Morse, ca. 1862
Oil on canvas on beaverboard, 14¾ x 11¼ (sight)
Museum of History and Technology, Smithsonian Institution, Washington, D.C.
[Figure 14]

THOMAS DOUGHTY (1793-1856)

11. HARPER'S FERRY FROM BELOW, ca. 1827
Wash on paper, 7 x 11
The Corcoran Gallery of Art, Washington, D.C.
[Figure 16]

Dimensions are in inches; height precedes width.

THOMAS COLE (1801-1848)

12. THE MOUNTAIN FORD: Study, ca. 1836
Pencil and chalk on toned paper, 9¾ x 6¾
The Corcoran Gallery of Art, Washington, D.C.
[Figure 17]

13. THE VOYAGE OF LIFE: Preliminary studies for CHILD-
HOOD, YOUTH, MANHOOD, OLD AGE, before 1839
Oil on wood panels, each ca. 12 x 14, framed together
Albany Institute of History and Art, Albany, New
York
[Figures 19, 20, 22, 25]

14. THE VOYAGE OF LIFE: MANHOOD: Study, ca. 1840
Oil on academy board, 12⅛ x 17
Smith College Museum of Art, Northampton, Massa-
chusetts
[Figure 23]

ASHER BROWN DURAND (1796-1886)

15. THANATOPSIS: Study, ca. 1850
Oil on canvas, 14⅞ x 20¾
Delaware Art Museum, Wilmington; gift of Titus C.
Geesey
[Figure 27]

FREDERIC EDWIN CHURCH (1826-1900)

16. THE OX-BOW: Study after Thomas Cole, 1844-1846
Oil on canvas, 20¼ x 30¼
Mr. and Mrs. Andrew S. Peters
[Figure 28]

17. SCENE IN THE CATSKILLS: Study, 1850
Oil on board, 12 x 15
Lyman Allyn Museum of Art, New London, Connecti-
cut
[Figure 30]

18. CHIMBORAZO: Study of the peak above clouds, 1853
Oil on cardboard, 12¼ x 19 (sight)
Cooper-Hewitt Museum of Design, Smithsonian Insti-
tution, New York City
[Figure 31]

19. CHIMBORAZO: Study of atmospheric effects, 1853
Oil on cardboard, 11 x 16 (sight)
Cooper-Hewitt Museum of Design, Smithsonian Insti-
tution, New York City
[Figure 32]

20. CHIMBORAZO: Study of the mountain, with house in
right foreground, 1853
Oil on cardboard, 11 x 17 (sight)
Cooper-Hewitt Museum of Design, Smithsonian Institution, New York City

21. COTOPAXI: Study of an eruption, 1857
Oil on board, 6½ x 10¾ (sight)
Cooper-Hewitt Museum of Design, Smithsonian Insti-
tution, New York City
[Figure 34]

22. COTOPAXI: Volcanic smoke and atmospheric effects,
1857
Oil on board, 7 x 11 (sight)
Cooper-Hewitt Museum of Design, Smithsonian Insti-
tution, New York City
[Figure 35]

23. NIAGARA FALLS: Study of the falls, 1856
Oil on board, 12¼ x 11 (sight)
Cooper-Hewitt Museum of Design, Smithsonian Insti-
tution, New York City
[Figure 37]

24. NIAGARA FALLS: Study of spray, 1856
Oil on board, 11 x 13½ (sight)
Cooper-Hewitt Museum of Design, Smithsonian Insti-
tution, New York City

THOMAS MORAN (1837-1926)

25. GRAND CANYON: Sketch with color notations, 1873
Pencil on paper, 10 x 14½ (sight)
Cooper-Hewitt Museum of Design, Smithsonian Insti-
tution, New York City
[Figure 40]

26. GRAND CANYON FROM POWELL PLATEAU: Study, 1873
Pencil and watercolor on toned paper, 7¼ x 10¼
(sight)
Cooper-Hewitt Museum of Design, Smithsonian Insti-
tution, New York City
[Figure 41]

27. MOUNTAIN OF THE HOLY CROSS: Sketch with color nota-
tions, 1874
Pencil on paper, 10½ x 14½ (sight)
Cooper-Hewitt Museum of Design, Smithsonian Insti-
tution, New York City
[Figure 43]

ELIHU VEDDER (1836-1923)

28. LE CASACCIE, OR BY THE WORLD FORGOT: Study in Umbria, 1867
Oil on cardboard, 12⅝ x 11⅝
Smith College Museum of Art, Northampton, Massachusetts; gift of the American Academy of Arts and Letters
[Figure 44]

JAMES GOODWYN CLONNEY (1812-1869)

29. MEXICAN NEWS: Preliminary study, ca. 1847
Pencil and chalk on paper, 9⁵/₁₆ x 11⅞
Munson-Williams-Proctor Institute, Utica, New York; gift of Hirshl and Adler Galleries
[Figure 45]

WILLIAM SIDNEY MOUNT (1807-1868)

30. DANCE OF THE HAYMAKERS and POWER OF MUSIC: Compositional studies, ca. 1845
Pencil on paper, 9 x 5½
The Museums at Stony Brook, Long Island, New York
[Figure 47]

31. EEL SPEARING AT SETAUKET: Preliminary study, ca. 1845
Oil on paper, 6½ x 7½
The Museums at Stony Brook, Long Island, New York
[Figure 48]

32. EEL SPEARING AT SETAUKET: Composition studies, ca. 1845
Pencil on paper, 9 x 5½
The Museums at Stony Brook, Long Island, New York
[Figure 49]

GEORGE CALEB BINGHAM (1811-1879)

33. FUR TRADERS DESCENDING THE MISSOURI: Study for the French trader, ca. 1845
Pencil and wash on paper, 11¾ x 9½
St. Louis Mercantile Library Association, Missouri; John How Collection
[Figure 53]

34. FUR TRADERS DESCENDING THE MISSOURI: Study for the half-breed son, ca. 1845
Pencil and wash on paper, 6⅞ x 9⅞
St. Louis Mercantile Library Association, St. Louis, Missouri; John How Collection
[Figure 52]

35. THE JOLLY FLATBOATMEN: Reclining figure seen from behind, ca. 1846
Pencil and wash on paper, 9¹⁵/₁₆ x 8⅛
St. Louis Mercantile Library Association, Missouri; John How Collection
[Figure 54]

36. THE JOLLY FLATBOATMEN: Study of a fiddler, ca. 1846
Pencil and wash on paper, 10 x 8⅜
St. Louis Mercantile Library Association, Missouri; John How Collection
[Figure 55]

37. COUNTRY ELECTION: Study of a toper, ca. 1852
Pencil and wash on paper, 11¹⁵/₁₆ x 9
St. Louis Mercantile Library Association, Missouri; John How Collection
[Figure 58]

38. COUNTRY ELECTION: Study of a drunken voter, ca. 1852
Pencil and wash on paper, 11⅜ x 9
St. Louis Mercantile Library Association, Missouri; John How Collection
[Figure 59]

39. COUNTRY ELECTION: Study of Revolutionary War veteran, ca. 1852
Pencil and wash on paper, 11⅝ x 9
St. Louis Mercantile Library Association, Missouri; John How Collection
[Figure 56]

EASTMAN JOHNSON (1824-1906)

40. CORN HUSKING: Figure studies, 1876
Pencil and watercolor on paper, 18¾ x 12¼
Free Library of Philadelphia, Pennsylvania; Rosenthal Collection of American Drawings
[Figure 60]

41. NANTUCKET INTERIOR: Study, 1876
Oil on panel, 6¾ x 10½
Wesleyan University, Center for the Humanities, Middletown, Connecticut; Ward Collection
[Figure 62]

42. THE REPRIMAND: Study of Capt. Charles Myrick, 1880
Charcoal on paper, 10¾ x 6¾
Free Library of Philadelphia, Pennsylvania; Rosenthal Collection of American Drawings
[Figure 63]

43. THE REPRIMAND: Composition study or variant, 1880
Oil on academy board, 17 x 11
Bernard and S. Dean Levy, Inc., New York City
[Figure 64]

WINSLOW HOMER (1836-1910)

44. THE LOOKOUT—ALL'S WELL: Study, ca. 1895
Crayon and gouache on paper, $12^7/_{16}$ x $13^{13}/_{16}$
Cooper-Hewitt Museum of Design, Smithsonian Institution, New York City
[Figure 65]

45. THE SIGNAL OF DISTRESS: Study of sailors manning a lifeboat, ca. 1890
Pencil and wash on paper, $13^7/_8$ x $11^5/_8$
Cooper-Hewitt Museum of Design, Smithsonian Institution, New York City
[Figure 67]

46. FISHERMEN WATCHING A STORM, or THE LIFE BRIGADE: Study of fishermen in oilskins, Tynmouth, England, 1881
Charcoal heightened with white on paper, $14^3/_4$ x $12^1/_{16}$
Cooper-Hewitt Museum of Design, Smithsonian Institution, New York City
[Figure 68]

THOMAS EAKINS (1844-1916)

47. THE ARTIST AND HIS FATHER HUNTING REED-BIRDS: Perspective study, ca. 1873
Pencil, pen and ink, and wash on paper, 31 x 47 (sight)
On extended loan to the Art Institute of Chicago
[Figure 69]

48. BETWEEN ROUNDS: Sketch of Billy Smith, the boxer, 1898
Oil on canvas, 20 x 16
Philadelphia Museum of Art, Pennsylvania; gift of Susan Macdowell Eakins and Mary A. Williams
[Figure 73]

49. COWBOYS IN THE BADLANDS: Study of dismounted cowhand, 1887
Oil on canvas, 24 x 20
Philadelphia Museum of Art, Pennsylvania; gift of Susan Macdowell Eakins and Mary A. Williams
[Figure 75]

50. WALT WHITMAN: Portrait study, 1887
Oil on panel, $5^1/_4$ x $5^1/_4$
Museum of Fine Arts, Boston, Massachusetts; Helen and Alice Colburn Fund
[Figure 103]

WILLIAM MERRITT CHASE (1849-1916)

51. THE COURT JESTER, or KEYING UP: Croquis, ca. 1875
Ink on paper, $8^3/_4$ x $4^1/_2$
Jackson Chase Storm, grandson of the artist
[Figure 76]

52. THE COURT JESTER, or KEYING UP: Graphic variant, ca. 1875
Etching, $5^3/_4$ x $3^1/_2$ (plate)
Dr. and Mrs. David Sellin

53. SERENADE TO A COCKATOO: Composition study with jester, ca. 1875
Oil on panel, 14 x 18
Jackson Chase Storm, grandson of the artist
[Figure 78]

FRANK DUVENECK (1848-1919)

54. WATER CARRIERS, VENICE: Study, ca. 1884
Pencil on paper, 12 x $6^1/_4$
Chapellier Galleries, New York City
[Figure 80]

WALTER SHIRLAW (1838-1909)

55. TONING THE BELL: Study for the violinist, ca. 1874
Ink wash on paper, $11^3/_4$ x $7^7/_8$ (sight)
The Corcoran Gallery of Art, Washington, D.C.
[Figure 82]

56. TONING THE BELL: Studies for the violinist and bellmaker, ca. 1874
Pencil on paper, 18 x 13 (sight)
Cooper-Hewitt Museum of Design, Smithsonian Institution, New York City
[Figure 83]

57. IN THE MOUNTAINS: Study for a decorative composition, 1875
Pencil on paper, $17^1/_4$ x $12^3/_4$ (sight)
Cooper-Hewitt Museum of Design, Smithsonian Institution, New York City

58. SHEEP SHEARING: Study, ca. 1876
Pencil on paper, 8 x 8 (sight)
Cooper-Hewitt Museum of Design, Smithsonian Institution, New York City
[Figure 85]

JOHN SINGER SARGENT (1856-1925)

59. OYSTER GATHERERS OF CANCALE, or EN ROUTE POUR LA
PECHE: Full study, or variant, ca. 1878
Oil on canvas, 16¼ x 23¾
Museum of Fine Arts, Boston, Massachusetts; gift of
Mary Appleton
[Figure 96]

60. EL JALEO: Study for the dancer, ca. 1882
Pencil and wash on paper, 10¼ x 5¼ (sight)
Lent by The Metropolitan Museum of Art; gift of
Mrs. Francis Ormand, 1950
[Figure 102]

JAMES ABBOTT McNIELL WHISTLER
(1834-1903)

61. COMPOSITION II: Early sketch, ca. 1865
Pencil on paper, 7⅛ x 8½
Munson-Williams-Proctor Institute, Utica, New York
[Figure 89]

62. ARRANGEMENT IN GREY AND BLACK NO. 2: Portrait study
of Thomas Carlyle, ca. 1872
Oil on canvas, 23¼ x 17¼
Haverford College, Haverford, Pennsylvania; gift of
C. W. Stock
[Figure 90]

CECILIA BEAUX (1855-1942)

63. LES DERNIERS JOURS D'ENFANCE: Composition study, ca.
1883
Oil on cardboard, 15¼ x 13¼
Pennsylvania Academy of the Fine Arts, Philadelphia;
gift of Henry S. Drinker, pictured here as a child
[Figure 106]

64. TWILIGHT CONFIDENCES: Study with Breton women and
haystack, 1888
Oil on canvas, 13¼ x 17¼
Pennsylvania Academy of the Fine Arts, Philadelphia;
gift of Henry S. Drinker
[Figure 108]

65. TWILIGHT CONFIDENCES: Study of Breton women, 1888
Oil on canvas, 15⅛ x 10⅝
Pennsylvania Academy of the Fine Arts, Philadelphia;
gift of Henry S. Drinker

66. TWILIGHT CONFIDENCES: Composition study with two
Breton women, 1888
Oil on canvas, 13¾ x 10¾
Pennsylvania Academy of the Fine Arts, Philadelphia;
gift of Henry S. Drinker
[Figure 109]

THEODORE ROBINSON (1852-1896)

67. TWO IN A BOAT: Composition study, ca. 1891
Photograph squared in pencil, 3¾ x 5
Ira Spanierman, Inc., New York City
[Figure 110]

MAURICE BRAZIL PRENDERGAST
(1861-1923)

68. THE BREEZY COMMON: ca. 1896/1897
Monotype, 7 x 9 (sight)
Dr. and Mrs. David Sellin
[Figure 113]

68a. THE BREEZY COMMON: Composition study, ca. 1896
Facsimile of a watercolor in a sketchbook dated 1899
in the Museum of Fine Arts, Boston, Massachusetts
[Figure 112]

WILLIAM MORRIS HUNT (1824-1879)

69. ANAHITA, or THE FLIGHT OF NIGHT: Study, ca. 1878
Gouache on paper, 16 x 36
William Morris Hunt II, grandson of the artist
[Figure 114]

JOHN LA FARGE (1835-1910)

70. COMMERCE: Composition study for the stained glass in
the house of William H. Vanderbilt on Fifth Avenue,
New York City, ca. 1885
Pencil and ink on paper, 9½ x 14⅞
The Corcoran Gallery of Art, Washington, D.C.
[Figure 116]

ELIHU VEDDER (1836-1923)

71. ROMA: Study for allegorical figure of Anima, ca. 1893
Crayon and chalk on brown paper, 15¼ x 11
Bowdoin College Museum of Art, Brunswick, Maine;
gift of the American Academy of Arts and Letters
[Figure 120]

KENYON COX (1856-1919)

72. VENICE: Figure study for the allegory of Painting, ca. 1893
Pencil on paper, 15½ x 19
Bowdoin College Museum of Art, Brunswick, Maine; gift of the Cooper-Hewitt Museum of Design, Smithsonian Institution
[Figure 121]

73. VENICE: Drapery study for the allegory of Painting, ca. 1893
Pencil on paper, 15 x 20½
Bowdoin College Museum of Art, Brunswick, Maine; gift of the Cooper-Hewitt Museum of Design, Smithsonian Institution
[Figure 122]

74. VENICE: Preliminary composition sketch, ca. 1893
Pencil on paper, 3⅞ x 6¼
Bowdoin College Museum of Art, Brunswick, Maine; gift of Col. Leonard Cox, Mrs. Caroline Cox Landsing, and Allyn Cox
[Figure 123]

75. VENICE: Composition sketch, 1893
Oil on canvas, 19¾ x 36
Bowdoin College Museum of Art, Brunswick, Maine; gift of Allyn Cox
[Figure 124]

EDWIN AUSTIN ABBEY (1852-1911)

76. THE PLAY SCENE FROM "HAMLET": Composition study, ca. 1897
Oil on canvas, 31¾ x 54
Yale University Art Gallery, New Haven, Connecticut; the Edwin Austin Abbey Memorial Collection
[Figure 127]

77. THE PLAY SCENE FROM "HAMLET": Study for the head of Ophelia
Oil on panel, 14 x 9⅝
Yale University Art Gallery, New Haven, Connecticut; the Edwin Austin Abbey Memorial Collection
[Figure 126]

JOHN SINGER SARGENT (1856-1925)

78. HELL: Preliminary study for a mural in the Boston Public Library, commissioned in 1890
Oil on canvas, 33¼ x 66¼ (lunette)
Smith College Museum of Art, Northampton, Massachusetts; gift of Mrs. Dwight W. Morrow
[Figure 128]

79. FRIEZE OF THE PROPHETS: Study for a mural in the Boston Public Library, 1890-1895
Oil on canvas, 22 x 28
Museum of Fine Arts, Boston, Massachusetts; gift of Mrs. Francis Ormond, the artist's sister
[Figure 129]

Suggested Reading

The artists represented in the exhibition are almost all subjects of major monographs or of exhibitions, the catalogs of which contain exhaustive bibliographies. Most of the paintings for which the studies were made are well documented in catalogs of the individual museums to which they belong.

Useful in putting the art works in historical perspective are a number of studies, including: John Baur, *American Painting in the Nineteenth Century: Main Trends and Movements* (New York: Praeger, 1953); James T. Flexner, *That Wilder Image: The Painting of America's Native School from Thomas Cole to Winslow Homer* (Boston/Toronto: Little, Brown & Co., 1962), reprinted in paperback by Dover Publications, 1970; Barbara Novak, *American Painting of the Nineteenth Century* (New York/Washington/London: Praeger, 1969).

The catalogs of a number of recent exhibitions contain up-to-date bibliographies, good commentaries, and visual material: *19th Century American Painting* (Metropolitan Museum of Art, New York, 1970); *The Düsseldorf Academy and the Americans* (High Art Museum, Atlanta, 1972); *American Pupils of Thomas Couture* (University of Maryland, 1970); *American Art in the Barbizon Mood* (National Collection of Fine Arts, Smithsonian Institution, 1975); *The Triumph of Realism* (Brooklyn Museum of Art, 1967); *Art for Architecture* (National Collection of Fine Arts, Smithsonian Institution, 1975).

The best gauge of nineteenth-century attitudes and goals is through the eyes of contemporaries. Essential tools are: William Dunlap, *History of the Rise and Progress of the Arts of Design in the United States* (New York, 1834), recently reprinted in paperback, Rita Weiss, ed. (New York: Dover Publications, 1969); Henry T. Tuckerman, *Book of the Artists* (New York, 1869); Clara E. Clement and Laurence Hutton, *Artists of the Nineteenth Century* (Boston, 1879); G. W. Sheldon, *American Painters*, 2d ed. (New York, 1880), containing the author's essays from *The Art Journal* (New York: D. Appleton & Co.), which was published in an American edition from 1875 through 1888, in itself a fine general index of taste.

Criticism by Earl Shinn (pseud., Edward Strahan), Robert F. Weir and his son, John W. Weir, is particularly useful because they were trained in art; and critic John Durand was the son of the painter Asher B. Durand. Part of the value of the criticism of men like Royal Cortissoz and Clarence Cook stems from the fact that they were not practical men, and thus were more tuned to pure theory. Sadakichi Hartmann, *A History of American Art* (Boston, 1901), summarized neatly the status of painting as seen from the turn of the century.